Critical Reasoning 1

Chad Troutwine · Markus Moberg · Cliff Smith · Mark Glenn

Co-Founders	Chad Troutwine
	Markus Moberg
Managing Editor	Mark Glenn
Director of Academic Programs	Brian Galvin
Interior Design	Lisa Johnson
	Miriam Lubow
Cover Design	Nick Mason
	Mike Miller
Contributing Editors	Joseph Dise
	David Lipowicz
	Lara Khouri
	Samuel Huang
	Jason Sun
Contributing Writer	Aaron Pond

VERITAS - Critical Reasoning I Notes

	S — Strengthen	W — Weaken	I — Inference	M — Method of Reasoning	M — Mimic the Reasoning	E — Explain the paradox	R — Roles of the Boldface
Focus	Author's conclusion – and key assumptions (unstated premises)	Author's conclusion – and gap in logic	Premises presented in the stimulus. Inference questions ask you to draw a conclusion based on information taken directly from the problem	Author's logic or argumentative technique	Logical pattern of the stimulus	You must select the answer choice that allows both parts of the stimulus to coexist. Focus on specifics of the paradox	Deconstruct the argument. Isolaet the conclusion. Recognize key premises. Evaluate whether the logic is valid or not. Look for common fallacies.
Answer	A premise. An answer must directly support the exact conclusion of the stimulus.	A premise	A deductive conclusion	A description of the author's logic	An argument (just like the stimulus)	Premise	Description of roles in the argument
GMAT Insider Solving Tips	The correct answer choice must provide new information relevant to the conclusion. Find the answer that supplies the missing premise (a key assumption). Remember that you don't need to prove the author's conclusion, just strengthen it.	Reflect on the gap in logic before looking at the answer choices. Look for the answer choice which exposes the gap in logic. Find a missing assumption / alternative explanation. Select the answer that supplies new information relevant to the conclusion. Remember: Your job is not disproving the author's argument – only need to cast doubt upon its validity. You need not disprove the author's conclusion, just weaken it.	Find the answer that must be true based on the stimulus. Eliminate any answer choices that are not necessarily true. Some arguments are expressed in bold terms and make categorical statements. Other arguments are carefully qualified with wording that limits their scope. When drawing an inference, recognize that the correct answer must be consistent with the scope and tone of the stimulus.	Focus on the argumentative approach, not the subject matter. Find the answer that is an accurate description of the logic. Eliminate answer choices that are inconsistent with the stimulus. The answers to Method of Reasoning questions often use the terminology of formal logic. Use a process of elimination to find the one answer that is an accurate description of the logic, rule out an answer choice if any detain mentioned is inconsistent with the scope of the stimulus.	Focus on the pattern of reasoning, not the subject matter. Find the answer that precisely matches the logic structure of the stimulus. If the stimulus contains flawed logic, eliminate any answers that are logically sound. If the stimulus is logically sound, eliminate any answers that contain flawed logic. On a Mimic the Reasoning question, you're the judge citing precedent for guidance: comparing the logic of the current case to that of a previous case. If the subject matter in the stimulus is repeated in an answer choice that answer choices is almost certainly incorrect. Remember that your job is to mimic the logic of the stimulus, not the subject matter.	Clearly identify the points that seem to contradict each other. Select the answer that explains how the seemingly contradictory positions are both true. Be sure to choose an answer that allows both parts of the stimulus to survive (do not contradict a premise)	Before reading the stimulus, scan the answer choices to note repeated or easily recognized role classificaitons. Deconstruct the argument: isolate the conclusion, identify the premises, evaluate the logic. Be wary of fallacies such as confusing necessary and sufficient conditions. Select the answer wich accurately describes the roles of both boldface portions.

Veritas Prep Expert Strategy – Attacking Critical Reasoning

1) Scan the question stem. Identify the question stem category (SWIMMER) for every question type. Do it quickly
2) Read the stimulus. You should look to spend about 2 minutes on each question (can vary based on the number of words and difficulty)
3) Read the question stem carefully. Based on the question category, keep in mind the following:

   a. Strengthening questions: anticipate what kind of missing premise would shore up the author's argument

   b. Weaken questions: reflect on what would undermine the author's argument

   c. Inference questions: look for the only answer choice that must be true based on the stimulus – the other answer choices may not be false, they are not necessarily true

   d. Method of Reasoning and Mimic the Reasoning questions: focus on logical structure, not the subject matter

   e. Explain the Paradox questions: consider what new information would reconcile the two sides of the paradox

   f. Roles questions: deconstruct the argument to determine the roles of the portions in boldface

Reminders: Note trigger words to properly identify the question type, focus on details, limit use of scratch paper on these questions, don't get intimidated by technical terms or distracted by convoluted language (main point is usually straight forward), positive mental attitude

GMAT Insider: When a question stem begins "Which of the following if true" or "Which of the following if valid", the answer choices are premises. The answers to three types of questions are premises: Strengthen, Weaken & Explain the paradox

A successful educational program is only as good as the people who teach it, and Veritas Prep is fortunate to have many of the world's finest GMAT instructors on its team.

Not only does that team know how to teach a strong curriculum, but it also knows how to help create one. This lesson book would not be possible without the hundreds of suggestions we have received from our talented faculty all across the world – from Seattle, Detroit, and Miami to London, Singapore, and Dubai. Their passion for excellence helped give birth to a new curriculum that is far better than what we could have created on our own.

Our students also deserve a very special thanks. Thousands of them have provided us with something priceless: enthusiastic feedback that has guided us in creating the most comprehensive GMAT preparation course available on the market today.

We therefore dedicate this revised lesson book to all Veritas Prep instructors and students who have tackled the GMAT and given us their valuable input along the way.

Table of Contents

Lesson 3 Introduction

In the Arguments lesson, you learned the fundamentals of GMAT Logic. Nowhere is comfort with GMAT Logic more necessary than on Critical Reasoning questions. Because this question type is new to most students, it can appear intimidating, but we will show you how to break these questions down into basic logical components. The Veritas Prep system, well-proven after years of use on real tests, will allow you to classify every question you'll ever come across. For each question classification, there is a tried and true solving strategy involving straightforward steps to take you to the correct answer.

Critical Reasoning

Directions: Analyze the situation on which each question is based, and then select the answer choice that is the most appropriate response to the question. No specialized knowledge of any particular field is required for answering the questions, and no knowledge of the terminologies and conventions of formal logic is presupposed.

Anatomy of a Critical Reasoning Problem

Dr. Larson: Sleep deprivation is the cause of many social ills, ranging from irritability to potentially dangerous instances of impaired decision making. Most people today suffer from sleep deprivation to some degree. Therefore we should restructure the workday to allow people flexibility in scheduling their work hours.

STIMULUS

Which of the following, if true, would most strengthen the medical doctor's argument?

QUESTION STEM

ANSWER CHOICES

(A)   The primary cause of sleep deprivation is overwork.

(B)   Employees would get more sleep if they had greater latitude in scheduling their work hours.

(C)   Individuals vary widely in the amount of sleep they require.

(D)   More people would suffer from sleep deprivation today than did in the past if the average number of hours worked per week had not decreased.

(E)   The extent of one's sleep deprivation is proportional to the length of one's workday.

2

Veritas Prep Methodology Critical Reasoning

Critical Reasoning Problems Deconstructed

> *GMAT Insider:* Critical Reasoning questions are designed to test your ability to think critically and evaluate arguments.

Critical Reasoning accounts for 12-14 of the 41 questions on the verbal section of the GMAT. Typically, each question contains a short passage of between 16 and 125 words (the stimulus), a question stem, and five answer choices. Questions appear in order of difficulty based on how well you are doing on the exam.

Critical Reasoning Question Stems Deconstructed

To perform well on Critical Reasoning questions, you need to properly identify the question category and apply the appropriate strategy based on your analysis. You identify question types by the question stem, not the stimulus that precedes or follows it.

Over the years the test-makers have created dozens of different question stems, but through exhaustive research Veritas Prep has determined that every Critical Reasoning GMAT question ever created falls into one of seven categories. Rather than merely address the major question types, we will cover all Critical Reasoning question types with one simple mnemonic device: SWIMMER.

> *GMAT Insider:* Because it is crucial for you to properly identify the question category on Critical Reasoning questions, you should read the question stem **before** reading the stimulus.

S:	Strengthen/support/assumption/premise
W:	Weaken/undermine/challenge/flaw/error/refute
I:	Inference/conclusion/deduction/must be true
M:	Method of reasoning
M:	Mimic the reasoning
E:	Explain the paradox
R:	Roles of bold-faced portions

Once you have learned to identify the question stem by category, you can find the correct answer choice with speed and confidence.

Strengthen

Strengthen questions can be posed in a variety of different ways. Trigger words include:

Strengthen
Justify/support
Assumption
Premise

Examples of Strengthen Question Stems:
Which of the following, if true, would most strengthen the conclusion drawn in the passage?

Which of the following, if true, most strongly supports the claim above about the manufacturer's profit?

Which of the following is an assumption that supports drawing the conclusion above from the reason given for that conclusion?

> *How Your Mind Works:* It is natural to want to dive into the stimulus first on Critical Reasoning questions. However, you will be given specific tasks to perform with the provided stimuli, and often these tasks will fall outside the scope of a surface-level understanding of the topic. Therefore, by reading the question stem first, your mind will already be attuned to the specific nature of your task and comprehension of the stimulus will come more easily.

No matter how the test-makers phrase the question stem, your strategy for all Strengthen questions is the same. All Strengthen questions will contain an argument in the stimulus (a conclusion and a set of premises). On Strengthen questions, the correct answer choice will always supply a missing premise that helps justify the argument's conclusion. Therefore, the correct answer choice must provide new information.

Remember: You do not need to prove the validity of the author's argument to strengthen it – you need only to add further support.

Strengthen Summary

Focus: Author's conclusion – and key assumptions (unstated premises), if any

Answer: A premise

Solving Tips: Select an answer that supplies new information relevant to the conclusion. Find the answer that supplies the missing premise (a key assumption). Remember that you do not need to prove the author's conclusion, just strengthen it.

> *GMAT Insider:* For each Critical Reasoning question type, picture yourself as playing a role in a courtroom. On a Strengthen question, you're the prosecutor putting forth evidence to help make your case.

1.   **Dr. Larson:** Sleep deprivation is the cause of many social ills, ranging from irritability to potentially dangerous instances of impaired decision making. Most people today suffer from sleep deprivation to some degree. Therefore we should restructure the workday to allow people flexibility in scheduling their work hours.

Which of the following, if true, would most strengthen the medical doctor's argument about sleep deprivation?

(A)   The primary cause of sleep deprivation is overwork.

(B)   Employees would get more sleep if they had greater latitude in scheduling their work hours.

(C)   Individuals vary widely in the amount of sleep they require.

(D)   More people would suffer from sleep deprivation today than did in the past if the average number of hours worked per week had not decreased.

(E)   The extent of one's sleep deprivation is proportional to the length of one's workday.

GMAT Insider: The correct answer on a Strengthen question must **directly** support the **exact** conclusion of the stimulus. If you have to go through multiple steps in your mind to make an answer support the conclusion, it is an incorrect, "tangential" answer choice.

Weaken

Trigger words include:

Weaken
Undermine
Cast doubt
Call into question
Jeopardize
Challenge
Err
Refute

Examples of Weaken Question Stems:
Which of the following most seriously weakens the argument?

Which of the following, if true, most undermines Danville Winery's response?

Your strategy for all Weaken questions should be the same regardless of how the question stem is phrased. The stimulus for any Weaken question contains an argument: a conclusion and a set of premises. The author's argument on a Weaken question is always incomplete. You should focus on the gap in logic in the stimulus and look for the answer choice that exposes it. You can weaken the argument by demonstrating that the author's conclusion does not flow logically from the premises, or by exposing the premises as incomplete or irrelevant.

Remember: Your job is not disproving the author's argument – you only need to cast doubt upon its validity.

Weaken Summary

Focus: Author's conclusion – and a gap in logic

Answer: A premise

Solving Tips: After reading the stimulus, reflect on the gap in logic before looking at the answers: If you were to write a letter to the editor, what would your topic be? Look for the answer choice which exposes the gap in logic. Find a missing assumption – perhaps an alternative explanation. Select an answer that supplies new information relevant to the conclusion. Remember that you need not disprove the author's conclusion, just weaken it.

2.   **Nate:** Recently a craze has developed for home juicers, $300 machines that separate the pulp of fruits and vegetables from the juice they contain. Outrageous claims are being made about the benefits of these devices: drinking the juice they produce is said to help one lose weight or acquire a clear complexion, to aid in digestion, and even to prevent cancer. But there is no indication that juice separated from the pulp of the fruit or vegetable has any properties that it does not have when unseparated. Save your money. If you want carrot juice, eat a carrot.

Which of the following, if true, most calls into question Nate's argument?

(A)   Most people find it much easier to consume a given quantity of nutrients in liquid form than to eat solid foods containing the same quantity of the same nutrients.

(B)   Drinking juice from home juicers is less healthy than is eating fruits and vegetables because such juice does not contain the fiber that is eaten if one consumes the entire fruit or vegetable.

(C)   To most people who would be tempted to buy a home juicer, $300 would not be a major expense.

(D)   Nate was a member of a panel that extensively evaluated early prototypes of home juicers.

(E)   Vitamin pills that supposedly contain nutrients available elsewhere only in fruits and vegetables often contain a form of those compounds that cannot be as easily metabolized as the varieties found in fruits and vegetables.

> *How Your Mind Works:* On Weaken questions, you must eliminate answer choices that have no effect on the argument. Beware, however, that of the remaining choices, one or more may **support** the author's argument. Remember that your mission is to **undermine** that argument. Do not allow yourself to be tricked into supporting the argument.

Inference

Trigger words include:

Inferred
Deduced
Gathered
Concluded
Is supported by
Must be true

Examples of Inference Question Stems:
Which of the following can be correctly inferred from the statements above?

Sharon's argument is structured to lead to which of the following as a conclusion?

Which of the following must be true on the basis of the statements in the advertisement above?

Inference questions ask you to draw a conclusion based on information taken directly from the problem. Because you must infer something based on statements contained in the stimulus, the correct answer choice for an Inference question must always be true. Thus, the other four answer choices are not necessarily true (although they don't have to be outright false).

Since only one answer choice must be true, Inference questions might appear to be the easiest you will face. To prevent that, the test-makers often use verbiage to obscure the logical structure of the stimulus and answer choices. The Veritas Prep GMAT Course will show you the common traps and teach you how to avoid them.

Remember: For Inference questions, only one answer choice must be true.

Inference Summary

Focus: Premises presented in the stimulus

Answer: A deductive conclusion

Solving tips: Find the answer that must be true based on the stimulus. Eliminate any answer choices that are not necessarily true.

> **GMAT Insider:** On an Inference question, you're the jury deciding what is true based on the evidence.

3.   Most antidepressant drugs cause weight gain. While dieting can help reduce the amount of weight gained while taking such antidepressants, some weight gain is unlikely to be preventable.

The information above most strongly supports which one of the following?

(A)   A physician should not prescribe any antidepressant drug for a patient if that patient is overweight.

(B)   People who are trying to lose weight should not ask their doctors for an anti-depressant drug.

(C)   At least some patients taking antidepressant drugs gain weight as a result of taking them.

(D)   The weight gain experienced by patients taking antidepressant drugs should be attributed to lack of dieting.

(E)   All patients taking antidepressant drugs should diet to maintain their weight.

GMAT Insider: Some arguments are expressed in bold terms and make categorical statements. Other arguments are carefully qualified with wording that limits their scope. When drawing an inference, recognize that the correct answer must be consistent with the scope and tone of the stimulus.

Method of Reasoning

Trigger phrases include:

Argumentative technique
Reasoning
Proceeds by

Examples of Method of Reasoning Question Stems:
The argument proceeds by...

Which of the following most accurately describes the essayist's method of defending the definition against the objection?

Method of Reasoning questions stems are rare. They have traditionally appeared in less than 5% of all GMAT Critical Reasoning questions. Because they are often difficult, these questions appear more frequently for those who are performing well on the GMAT. When Method of Reasoning questions appear, the format is always the same: the stimulus presents one or more arguments and you must characterize the author's method of reasoning.

Remember: On Method of Reasoning questions, focus on the logic of the argument, not its subject matter.

Method of Reasoning Summary

Focus:	Author's logic or argumentative technique
Answer:	A description of the author's logic
Solving Tips:	Focus on the argumentative approach, not the subject matter. Find the answer that is an accurate description of the logic. Eliminate answer choices that are inconsistent with the stimulus.

> *GMAT Insider:* On a Method of Reasoning question, you're the courtroom reporter describing how the case has been made.

> *GMAT Insider:* The answers to Method of Reasoning questions often use the terminology of formal logic. The directions for critical reasoning state: "No knowledge of the terminology and conventions of formal logic is presupposed." Thus you can determine the correct answer even if the argumentative techniques described are unfamiliar to you. Use a process of elimination to find the one answer that is an accurate description of the logic; rule out an answer choice if any detail mentioned is inconsistent with the scope of the stimulus.

4.   **Imran:** The only way for a company to be successful, after emerging from bankruptcy, is to produce the same goods or services that it did before going bankrupt. It is futile for such a company to try to learn a whole new business.

Weber: Wrong. The Kelton Company was a major mining operation that went into bankruptcy. On emerging from bankruptcy, Kelton turned its mines into landfills and is presently a highly successful waste-management company.

Weber uses which one of the following argumentative techniques in countering Imran's argument?

(A)   He presents a counterexample to a claim.

(B)   He offers an alternative explanation for a phenomenon.

(C)   He supports a claim by offering a developed and relevant analogy.

(D)   He undermines a claim by showing that it rests on an ambiguity.

(E)   He establishes a conclusion by excluding the only plausible alternative to that conclusion.

Habits of Great Test Takers:
I like to think of Critical Reasoning as a grown up version of the baby block game, the one where the baby has to put the 3D geometric shapes in the right slot. We've all seen, at one time or another, a baby trying to force a sphere into the cube slot. If he pushes hard enough, it will eventually go in, but that's not where it belongs. What we do at Veritas Prep is teach you how to distinguish the critical reasoning "shapes" and to recognize which shape the questions are asking for. Once you've mastered these skills, Critical Reasoning becomes almost as simple as the baby block game.

—Travis Sorensen, MARYLAND

Mimic the Reasoning

Trigger phrases include:

Parallels
Logical structure
Most similar to
Pattern of reasoning

Examples of Mimic the Reasoning Question Stems:
The pattern of reasoning above most closely parallels that in which of the following?

The argument is most parallel, in its logical structure, to which one of the following?

Mimic the Reasoning questions are extremely rare on the GMAT. A staple on tests like the LSAT, they have historically appeared in less than 2% of all GMAT Critical Reasoning questions. When they appear, the format is always the same: the correct answer choice precisely matches the logic structure of the stimulus. If the stimulus contains flawed logic, then the correct answer choice will be the one (and only one) flawed in exactly the same way. If the stimulus is logically sound, you must find a logically sound answer choice (crafted in the same fashion as the stimulus).

Mimic the Reasoning Summary

Focus: Logic pattern of the stimulus

Answer: An argument (just like the stimulus)

Solving Tips: Focus on the pattern of reasoning, not
                 the subject matter. Find the answer
                 that precisely matches the logic structure
                 of the stimulus. If the stimulus contains
                 flawed logic, eliminate any answers that
                 are logically sound. If the stimulus is
                 logically sound, eliminate any answers that
                 contain flawed logic.

5.   It is inaccurate to say that a diet high in refined sugar cannot cause adult-onset diabetes, since a diet high in refined sugar can make a person overweight, and being overweight can predispose a person to adult-onset diabetes.

The argument above is most parallel, in its logical structure, to which of the following?

(A)   It is inaccurate to say that being in cold air can cause a person to catch a cold, since colds are caused by viruses, and viruses flourish in warm, crowded places.

(B)   It is accurate to say that no airline flies from Halifax to Washington. No airline offers a direct flight, although some airlines have flights from Halifax to Boston and others have flights from Boston to Washington.

(C)   It is correct to say that over-fertilization is the primary cause of lawn disease, since fertilizer causes lawn grass to grow rapidly and rapidly growing grass has little resistance to disease.

(D)   It is incorrect to say that inferior motor oil cannot cause a car to get poorer gasoline mileage, since inferior motor oil can cause engine valve deterioration, and engine valve deterioration can lead to poorer gasoline mileage.

(E)   It is inaccurate to say that Alexander the Great was a student of Plato; Alexander was a student of Aristotle and Aristotle was a student of Plato.

Explain the Paradox

Trigger words include:

Explain
Paradox
Resolve
Apparent discrepancy
Reconcile

Examples of the Explain Question Stems:
Which of the following, if true, most helps to resolve the apparent paradox outlined above?

Which of the following, if true, best explains the discrepancy outlined above?

Explain questions ask you to explain what appears to be a paradox. Typically, the stimulus presents seemingly contradictory positions. Your job is to select the only answer choice that reconciles the two positions.

Remember: You must select the answer choice that allows **both** parts of the stimulus to coexist.

Explain the Paradox Summary

Focus: Specifics of the paradox

Answer: Premise

Solving Tips: Clearly identify the points that seem to contradict each other. Select the answer that explains how the seemingly contradictory positions are both true. Be sure to choose an answer that allows both parts of the stimulus to survive (do not contradict a premise).

6.	Scientists agree that ingesting lead harms young children. More lead paint remains in older apartment buildings than newer ones because the use of lead paint was common until only two decades ago. Yet these same scientists also agree that laws requiring the removal of lead paint from older apartment buildings will actually increase the amount of lead that children living in older apartment buildings ingest.

Which of the following, if true, most helps to resolve the apparent discrepancy in the scientists' beliefs?

(A)	Lead-free paints contain substances that make them as harmful to children as lead paint is.

(B)	The money required to finance the removal of lead paint from apartment walls could be spent in ways more likely to improve the health of children.

(C)	Other sources of lead in older apartment buildings are responsible for most of the lead that children living in these buildings ingest.

(D)	Removing lead paint from walls disperses a great deal of lead dust, which is more easily ingested by children than is paint on walls.

(E)	Many other environmental hazards pose greater threats to the health of children than does lead paint.

Roles of Portions in Boldface

Questions on Roles are easy to recognize since the question stem is always worded the same way, and the stimulus always has two portions highlighted in boldface.

Example of Roles of Portions in Boldface:
The two portions in boldface play which of the following roles?

The test makers introduced the roles type of question in 2005. After taking the GMAT, students typically report that they faced one or two of this form of critical reasoning question. Roles questions are not common, but every student should expect to see at least one critical reasoning question of this type on the GMAT.

Roles questions draw heavily on your understanding of argument structure. The correct answer describes the roles of portions in boldface. The descriptions may be generic (for example, "the first portion is evidence that supports the argument") or they may be specific to the subject matter (for example, "the first is a pattern of cause and effect that the consumer advocate argues will be repeated in the case at issue"). To select the correct answer choice, deconstruct the argument using the information covered in the Arguments lesson. Isolate the conclusion. Recognize key premises. Evaluate whether the logic is valid or not. Look for common fallacies (logical errors).

Remember: The correct answer must accurately describe the roles of **both** portions in boldface.

> *GMAT Insider:* On a Roles question, you're again the courtroom reporter, but here you are identifying different parts of the case.

Roles of Portions in Boldface Summary

Focus: The argument's logic, and specifically the roles of portions in boldface

Answer: Descriptions of roles in the argument

Solving tips: Before reading the stimulus, scan the answer choices to note repeated or easily recognized role classifications. Deconstruct the argument: isolate the conclusion, identify the premises, evaluate the logic. Be wary of fallacies such as confusing necessary and sufficient conditions. Select the answer which accurately describes the roles of **both** boldface portions.

7.   **Some analysts predict that next year will see total worldwide sea shipping tonnage increase by 2% over the current year.** However, captains of freight ships generally expect that worldwide shipping tonnage will decrease next year. **At issue is the amount of freight that will be shifted from sea ships to freight airplanes as compared to growth in the overall demand for freight transport.** The analysts believe growth in demand will outstrip the shift to freight airplanes; the ship captains believe the opposite.

The two portions in **boldface** play which of the following roles?

(A)   The first portion is evidence that supports a position; the second portion is a position that is not necessarily true based on the evidence.

(B)   The first portion represents one of two opposed positions; the second portion describes the underlying reason for the difference in position.

(C)   The first portion represents one of two opposed positions; the second portion is evidence in support of that position.

(D)   The first portion is evidence that supports a position; the second portion is evidence that supports an opposed position.

(E)   The first portion represents one of two opposed positions; the second portion represents the opposing position.

Veritas Prep Expert Strategy Attacking Critical Reasoning

- First, scan the question stem. Identify the question stem category (SWIMMER) for every question, but do it quickly.

- Next, read the stimulus. In the advanced lessons in the Veritas Prep GMAT Course, you should become more conscious of time. You should look to spend about two minutes on each question (though that can vary based on the number of words and relative difficulty of the stimulus). For now, focus on reading carefully and critically.

- Third, read the question stem carefully. Based on the question category, keep in mind the following:

    o Strengthen questions: anticipate what kind of missing premise would shore up the author's argument.

    o Weaken questions: reflect on what would undermine the author's argument.

    o Inference questions: look for the only answer choice that must be true based on the stimulus – the other answers choices may not be false, they are just not necessarily true.

    o Method of Reasoning and Mimic the Reasoning questions: focus on logical structure, not subject matter.

    o Explain the Paradox questions: consider what new information would reconcile the two sides of the paradox.

    o Roles questions: deconstruct the argument to determine the roles of the portions in boldface.

> **GMAT Insider:**
> **A Note About The Word "Support"**
> The word "support" can be a trigger word for Strengthen questions or Inference questions, depending on how it is used.
>
> Some questions ask which answer is supported by the stimulus, for example: "The information above supports which of the following?" In this case, your task is to find the conclusion that is supported by the premises in the stimulus. This is an Inference question.
>
> Other questions ask which answer supports the argument presented in the stimulus, for example: "Which of the following statements best supports the author's conclusion?" For such questions, your task is to find the premise that helps justify the author's main point. This is a Strengthen question.
>
> If the question stem includes the word "support," consider whether the support comes from the answer (a Strengthen question) or from the stimulus (an Inference question).

- Finally, read each answer choice and select the correct one. After today, you will see why we devoted so much time to identifying premises and conclusions in Arguments.

Additional Critical Reasoning Reminders

- Note important trigger words to properly identify the question stem category.

- Focus on the details.

- **Limit** use of scratch paper on these questions.

- Do **not** get intimidated by technical terms or distracted by convoluted language. The main point of the passage is usually straightforward.

- Maintain a positive mental attitude. Focus on SWIMMER and strategic thinking.

- In a later lesson, you will learn that scope and tone are crucial for success with reading comprehension questions. Scope and tone impact critical reasoning, too. Any answer choice that is too broad (or narrow) relative to the stimulus is wrong. We will identify examples throughout the course.

Critical Reasoning Summarized

- Accounts for 12 -14 of the 41 questions on the verbal section of the GMAT.

- Stimuli range in length from 16 to 125 words.

- Question stems fall into the following categories: Strengthen, Weaken, Inference, Method of Reasoning, Mimic the Reasoning, Explain, Roles (or "SWIMMER") – the secret to your success on critical reasoning is to properly identify the question stem and apply the appropriate strategy.

- Your task is to (1) read the question stem and identify its category, (2) carefully read the stimulus, (3) re-read the question stem and, if applicable, anticipate the correct answer choice, and (4) read all of the answer choices, selecting the correct one as dictated by the question stem category.

In-Class Drill

Identify the Question Category, using SWIMMER:

1.   Which of the following is a presupposition of the argument above?

2.   Which one of the following is a logical conclusion based on the information above?

3.   Which one of the following, if true, best reconciles the discrepancy described above?

4.   The argument assumes which one of the following?

5.   Which one of the following most accurately expresses the main point of the argument?

6.   Which one of the following can be correctly inferred from the argument above?

7.   Which one of the following is supported by the argument above?

8.   Which one of the following proposals, if implemented together with the proposal made above, would improve the prospects for achieving the stated objective?

9.   Which one of the following techniques of argument does the author use above?

10.   Which of the following, if true, is most damaging to the statement above?

11.   In terms of its logical structure, the remark above most closely resembles which
        of the following?

12.   Which of the following arguments makes the same logical error as the one
        described by the author above?

13.   Which one of the following, if true, most seriously weakens the argument made
        above that an unequal distribution of wealth is necessary for the accumulation
        of capital?

14.   Which one of the following is most like the argument above in its logical structure?

15.   The author implies which of the following?

16.   Which of the following would cast the Veterans Administration's argument into
        the most serious doubt?

17.   Which of the following conclusions can be drawn from the information above?

18.   The author uses which of the following methods of persuasion?

19.   From which one of the following does the conclusion logically follow?

20.   The two portions in boldface play which of the following roles?

21.   Which of the following most closely parallels the reasoning used in the
        argument above?

22.   Which of the following, if true, would most greatly strengthen the
        argument above?

23.   Which one of the following is an assumption on which the conclusion of the
        argument depends?

24.   Which one of the following is the most effective criticism of the newscaster's reasoning?

25.   Which one of the following most closely parallels the flawed reasoning in the argument above?

26.   Which of the following is the most pertinent criticism of the argument above?

27.   Which of the following, if true, does most to justify this apparently paradoxical belief?

28.   If all of the statements above are true, which of the following must also be true on the basis of them?

29.   The scientist's conclusion about the 1908 explosion assumes which of the following?

30.   Which of the following could individually constitute reasonable explanations of the paradox presented above?

> *Habits of Great Test Takers*: For each book I keep a list of problems to re-do. Three types of problems end up on the re-do list: 1) Problems I got wrong, 2) Problems I got right but for the wrong reasons (guessed, got lucky, etc), and 3) Problems that I got right but that took me too long to complete. Don't underestimate the value of re-doing a problem that you had trouble with the first time around (usually I wait at least a week before trying it again). You'll be amazed at how often you make the same mistake twice if you don't fully understand something!
> —Heather Speller, New Haven

Assorted Problems

8.   The television show *The Office* was not widely watched until it was scheduled for Tuesday evenings immediately following *My Name is Earl*, a popular comedy. During the year after the move, *The Office* was consistently one of the ten most watched shows on television. Since *The Office* moved to Thursday evenings, however, it has been watched by far fewer people. We must conclude that *The Office* was widely watched before the move to Thursday evenings because it followed *My Name is Earl* and not because people especially liked it.

Which one of the following, if true, most strengthens the argument?

(A)   *The Office* has been on the air for four seasons, but *My Name is Earl* has been on the air for only three seasons.

(B)   The show that replaced *The Office* on Tuesdays has persistently had a low number of viewers in the Tuesday time slot.

(C)   The show that now follows *My Name is Earl* has double the number of viewers it had before being moved.

(D)   After its recent move to Thursday, *The Office* was aired at the same time as the second most popular cable show on television.

(E)   Situational comedies like *The Office* and *My Name is Earl* have recently begun losing market share to reality programming.

9.   Raisins are made by drying grapes in the sun. Although some of the sugar in the grapes is caramelized in the process, nothing is added. Moreover, the only thing removed from the grapes is the water that evaporates during the drying, and water contains no calories or nutrients. The fact that raisins contain more iron per food calorie than grapes do is thus puzzling.

Which one of the following, if true, most helps to explain why raisins contain more iron per calorie than do grapes?

(A)   Since grapes are bigger than raisins, it takes several bunches of grapes to provide the same amount of iron as a handful of raisins does.

(B)   Caramelized sugar cannot be digested, so its calories do not count toward the food calorie content of raisins.

(C)   The body can absorb iron and other nutrients more quickly from grapes than from raisins because of the relatively high water content of grapes.

(D)   Raisins, but not grapes, are available year-round, so many people get a greater share of their yearly iron intake from raisins than from grapes.

(E)   Raisins are often eaten in combination with other iron-containing foods, while grapes are usually eaten by themselves.

10. There are those who complain that municipal libraries are outdated and unnecessary. **These same people object to the tax dollars spent funding municipal libraries.** However, these people are missing out on a simple pleasure: reading a great book. Taken this way, **libraries are truly wonderful resources worthy of public funding.**

The two **boldface** portions play which of the following roles?

(A) The first is a generalization accepted by the author as true; the second is a consequence that follows from the truth of that generalization.

(B) The first is evidence that supports one of two contradictory points of view; the second is the second point of view.

(C) The first is a commonly held point of view; the second is support for that point of view.

(D) The first is one of two contradictory points of view; the second is the other point of view.

(E) The first concedes a consideration that weighs against the viewpoint of the author; the second is that viewpoint.

8)

√NOT   S   A   ~~B~~   Ⓒ   ~~D~~ ~~E~~

X 9) Explain

Ⓐ   ~~B~~   ~~C~~   ~~D~~ ~~E~~

Iron for food calorie

11) conclusion

    I   ~~A~~   ~~B~~   Ⓒ   ~~D~~ ~~E~~

Explain   x   bright

question   didn't breakdown qs

X 10)   outdated → some people object

worth of pub findg

~~A~~   B   ~~C~~   D   Ⓔ

11)   A   B   C   D   E

Explain Par

11.   When astronomers observed the comet Steinman-Arnett 3 becoming 1,000 times brighter in September 1995, they correctly hypothesized that its increased brightness was a result of the comet's breaking up. When comets break up, they emit large amounts of gas and dust, becoming visibly brighter as a result. However, their observations did not reveal comet Steinman-Arnett 3 actually breaking into pieces until November 1995, even though telescopes were trained on it throughout the entire period.

Which of the following, if true, most helps to resolve the apparent conflict in the situation above?

(A)   Comets often do not emit gas and dust until several weeks after they have begun to break up.

(B)   The reason comets become brighter when they break up is that the gas and dust that they emit refract light.

(C)   Gas and dust can be released by fissures in a comet, even if the comet is not broken all the way through.

(D)   The amount of gas and dust emitted steadily increased during the period from September through November.

(E)   The comet passed close to the sun during this period and the gravitational strain caused it to break up.

12. In one study engineering students who prepared for an exam by using toothpicks and string did no worse than similar students who prepared by using an expensive computer with sophisticated graphics. In another study, military personnel who trained on a costly high-tech simulator performed no better on a practical exam than did similar personnel who trained using an inexpensive cardboard model. So one should not always purchase technologically advanced educational tools.

Which of the following principles, if valid, most helps to justify the reasoning above?

(A) One should use different educational tools to teach engineering to civilians than are used to train military personnel.

(B) High-tech solutions to modern problems are ineffective unless implemented by knowledgeable personnel.

(C) Spending large sums of money on educational tools is at least as justified for nonmilitary training as it is for military training.

(D) One should not invest in expensive teaching aids unless there are no other tools that are less expensive and at least as effective.

(E) One should always provide students with a variety of educational materials so that each student can find the materials that best suit that student's learning style.

GMAT Insider: When the question stem begins "Which of the following, if true," or "Which of the following, if valid," the answer choices are premises. The answers to three types of questions are premises: Strengthen, Weaken, and Explain.

13. More and more computer programs that provide solutions to mathematical problems in engineering are being produced, and it is thus increasingly unnecessary for practicing engineers to have thorough understanding of fundamental mathematical principles. Consequently, in training engineers who will work in industry, less emphasis should be placed on mathematical principles, so that space in the engineering curriculum will be available for other important subjects.

Which of the following, if true, most seriously weakens the argument given for the recommendation above?

(A) The effective use of computer programs that provide solutions to mathematical problems in engineering requires an understanding of fundamental mathematical principles.

(B) Many of the computer programs that provide solutions to mathematical problems in engineering are already in routine use.

(C) Development of composites and other such new materials has meant that the curriculum for engineers who will work in industry must allow time for teaching the properties of these materials.

(D) Most of the computer programs that provide solutions to mathematical problems in engineering can be run on the types of computers available to most engineering firms.

(E) The engineering curriculum already requires that engineering students be familiar with and able to use a variety of computer programs.

14. Opponents of peat harvesting in this country argue that it would alter the ecological balance of our peat-rich wetlands and that, as a direct consequence of this, much of the country's water supply would be threatened with contamination. But this cannot be true, for in Ireland, where peat has been harvested for centuries, the water supply is not contaminated. We can safely proceed with the harvesting of peat.

Which one of the following, if true, most strengthens the argument?

(A) Over hundreds of years, the ecological balance of all areas changes slowly but significantly, sometimes to the advantage of certain flora and fauna.

(B) The original ecology of the peat-harvesting areas of Ireland was virtually identical to that of the undisturbed wetlands of this country.

(C) The activities of the other industries in coming years are likely to have adverse effects on the water supply of this country.

(D) The peat resources of this country are far larger than those of some countries that successfully harvest peat.

(E) The peat-harvesting industry of Ireland has been able to supply most of that country's fuel for generations.

15. **Opponent of offshore oil drilling:** The projected benefits of drilling new oil wells in certain areas in the outer continental shelf are not worth the risk of environmental disaster. The oil already being extracted from these areas currently provides only 4 percent of our country's daily oil requirement, and the new wells would only add one-half of 1 percent.

Proponent of offshore oil drilling: Don't be ridiculous! You might just as well argue that new farms should not be allowed, since no new farm could supply the total food needs of our country for more than a few minutes.

The drilling proponent's reply to the drilling opponent proceeds by:

(A) Offering evidence in support of drilling that is more decisive than is the evidence offered by the drilling opponent.

(B) Claiming that the statistics cited as evidence by the drilling opponent are factually inaccurate.

(C) Pointing out that the drilling opponent's argument is a misapplication of a frequently legitimate way of arguing.

(D) Citing as parallel to the argument made by the drilling opponent an argument in which the conclusion is strikingly unsupported.

(E) Proposing a conclusion that is more strongly supported by the drilling opponent's evidence than is the conclusion offered by the drilling opponent.

16. To get into a top MBA program **one must have five years of work experience and a 90th percentile GMAT score**. Alexis has a 95th percentile GMAT score and five years of experience in the work force, so **Alexis must be accepted into a top MBA program.**

The two portions in **boldface** play which of the following roles?

(A) The first is a piece of evidence; the second is a conclusion that must be true based on the evidence presented.

(B) The first is a piece of evidence; the second is a conclusion that is not necessarily true based on the evidence.

(C) The first is a conclusion that follows from the evidence; the second is a piece of evidence.

(D) The first is a conclusion that is not necessarily true based on the evidence; the second is a piece of evidence.

(E) The first is the conclusion of the author; the second is a cause-and-effect relationship that supports the conclusion.

17.   On average, plowed land erodes away at slightly more than 1 millimeter per year, while new soil builds up at about 0.2 millimeters per year. As a result, continually cultivated soil will become exhausted in the space of several hundred years, unless no-till agriculture is practiced. No-till agriculture is a method in which crop stubble remains in place and a special drill inserts the seeds into the soil. However, only about 16 percent of cultivated areas in the United States use this method.

Which of the following is best supported by the information above?

(A)   Although the advance of farming technology has made no-till agriculture available to wealthy farmers, such methods are financially impractical for many American farmers.

(B)   If the United States does not utilize means that replenish or reuse exhausted soil, it must eventually find other ways of getting agricultural products.

(C)   Agricultural industries that do not require plowing – such as dairy or chicken farms – are not affected by topsoil erosion.

(D)   If 5 out of 6 of all American farms were to practice no-till agriculture, the United States would produce enough agricultural products to meet domestic demand for several hundred years.

(E)   Hydroponic farming (farming without soil) would solve the United States' land erosion problem.

18.   Acid rain, caused by high levels of sulfur dioxide and mercury trapped in global air currents, affects one-third of China's territory. Coal-fired power plants are notorious for emitting large quantities of these pollutants. To combat the problem, the Chinese national government has set aggressive environmental goals for the next 5 years. These goals include a 20 percent improvement in energy efficiency and a pledge that by the end of the 5 years, 10 percent of the nation's energy will come from renewable resources such as hydroelectric or wind power.

Which of the following, if true, is the best criticism of the Chinese government's strategy as a method for achieving a reduction in acid rain?

(A)   Some forms of air pollution, such as heavy particulate fumes, would not be affected by the suggested energy improvements.

(B)   Once the changes have been implemented, the actual reduction in acid rain would vary from region to region.

(C)   The goals would be forced on every region in China, including those that have no problems with acid rain.

(D)   Acid rain is also caused by other factors, such as volcanic eruptions or pollution from neighboring countries, over which China has no control.

(E)   Regional Chinese officials tend to ignore environmental regulations in order to meet aggressive economic requirements imposed on their regions' industries.

19.   Despite radical fluctuations during the previous decade, unit labor costs (that is, the average labor cost per unit produced manufacturers' average) in country Q have remained unchanged for the last several years. However, during this period of stabilization, the average hourly wage of manufacturing laborers has increased by 7.2%.

        Which of the following, if true, most helps to explain why the increase in hourly manufacturing labor cost of manufacturing labor in country Q has not led to an increase in average unit labor cost?

(A)   Inflation has caused the purchase price of goods manufactured in country Q to increase at the same rate.

(B)   The increase in the average cost of manufacturing labor per hour has occurred despite decreases in the raw material costs.

(C)   During the same period, manufacturing productivity (units produced per laborer per hour) increased at the same rate as did wages.

(D)   In the last few years, there has been a shift in the economy of country Q, leading to more service-oriented jobs and fewer manufacturing jobs.

(E)   When the hourly compensation rate increases, it is possible to hire workers with greater skill levels.

20.   The search for NEOs (or "Near-Earth Objects") has intensified greatly within the last few years with the emergence of a virtual army of amateur astronomers. By combining their observations into a single database at the Smithsonian Astrophysical Observatory, "backyard scientists" are capable of accurately determining the orbits and motions of asteroids that could hit the Earth. Indeed, in recent years much of the burden for accurately evaluating the risks posed by NEOs has been shouldered by amateur astronomers. Therefore, we should reserve larger, professional telescopes for uses other than finding NEOs.

Which of the following, if true, most seriously weakens the argument above?

(A)   Because of their numbers, amateur astronomers as a group are much more efficient than are individual professional telescopes at accurately determining NEO orbits.

(B)   Because large telescopes are often controlled by governments or institutions, professional scientists do not always have full discretion to use these telescopes any way they would like.

(C)   Most amateur astronomers do not have any professional training in astronomy.

(D)   NASA has set a goal of finding at least 90% of the estimated 1,000 NEOs larger than 1 kilometer in diameter.

(E)   Amateur astronomers primarily provide follow-up observations after NEO discoveries have been made by the use of larger, computerized telescopes.

21.   Highways 24 and 105 each have relatively equal traffic loads, meaning their average daily vehicle counts are virtually equal. According to records maintained by the State Department of Transportation, Highway 24 had fewer vehicle accidents last year than did Highway 105. Therefore, driving on Highway 24 is safer than driving on Highway 105.

Which of the following, if true, would most strengthen the conclusion above?

(A)   Highway 105 runs through lowlands notorious for poor visibility due to heavy fog, while Highway 24 does not.

(B)   More than twice as many highway patrol officers are assigned to Highway 105 than to Highway 24.

(C)   The emergency rooms of the hospital located along Highway 105 report considerably more injuries than do those of the hospital near Highway 24.

(D)   Highway 24 had more fatal accidents than Highway 105 last year.

(E)   Highway 105 was built with traditional asphalt, while Highway 24 was built with a newer, more inexpensive asphalt substitute.

22. From 1994 to 2001, violent crime in New York City steadily decreased by over 50%, from a rate of 1,861 violent crimes per 100,000 people in 1994 down to 851 violent crimes per 100,000 people in 2001. Criminologist have partially attributed this drop to proactive policing tactics such as "Broken Window Policing," wherein city officials immediately fixed small acts of vandalism and, as a result, lowered other types of criminal behavior. During this same period, the rate of violent crime steadily decreased in the United States by 28% (down to 500 violent crimes per 100,000 people).

Which of the following conclusions is best supported by the information above?

(A) The decrease in the total crime rate in the United States caused the decrease in New York City's crime rate.

(B) New York City spends more per capita on law enforcement than does the rest of the United States.

(C) If the rest of the United States were to adopt law enforcement procedures similar to those of New York City, national violent crime rates would continue to fall.

(D) Between 1994 and 2001, the violent crime rate in New York City was consistently higher than the national average.

(E) The violent crime rate in New York City will soon be below the national average.

23. After Company K released its low-fat butter substitute for the first time into European markets, it found that it was unable to achieve any appreciable market share. To combat this problem, Company K re-released the product under a new name with great fanfare and a substantial marketing budget, calling it the "new low-fat alternative to butter."

Which of the following, if true, casts the most doubt on the effectiveness of the solution proposed above?

(A) Satisfactory taste and low-fat content are believed in many European countries to be entirely contradictory.

(B) The market for yellow fats such as margarine and butter has been slowly shrinking in many European countries due to the emergence of specialized cheese spreads.

(C) Company K could only feasibly maintain such a marketing budget for 10 to 12 months, after which it would have to downscale the campaign.

(D) After Company K attempted a similar marketing strategy in South America, sales of the new product greatly increased.

(E) In Denmark, the new low-fat butter substitute achieved a market share of 15% within the first year – without any massive marketing campaign.

24. Some scientists believe that sugar causes a specific type of pancreatic cancer. They have found that people who consume at least 2 carbonated drinks containing sugar per day have a 90% higher rate of pancreatic cancer than those who drink the same number of diet drinks per day. Therefore, if we were to substitute diet drinks for regular soda pop, it would considerably reduce our chances of getting pancreatic cancer.

Which of the following, if true, most seriously weakens the argument above?

(A) Many diet drinks contain artificial sweeteners called cyclamates, which have been known to cause intestinal and bladder cancer in laboratory studies.

(B) Statistically, people who consume several sugared drinks a day are also the least likely to maintain a regular exercise regimen. It has been shown that regular exercise is a factor in reducing many types of cancer, including pancreatic.

(C) People who generally avoid sugared beverages also tend to avoid sugar in other parts of their diet.

(D) Diet drinks have actually been linked to a higher risk of weight gain.

(E) The study showed that the increase in the rate of pancreatic cancer remained the same whether the person drank 2 or 5 sugared drinks per day on average.

25.   A team of scientists has recently linked intense tropospheric lightning storms in the Ethiopian Highlands to the formation of hurricanes along the Atlantic seaboard. The lightning activity, they claim, is so powerful that it creates atmospheric waves across the Sahara that are conclusively linked to many Atlantic hurricanes. However, in the Caribbean, where these atmospheric waves could never reach, hurricane activity is even greater than along the Atlantic seaboard.

Which of the following statements draws the most reliable conclusion from the information above?

(A)   Ethiopian lightning storms cannot be the only factor that affects the formation of hurricanes.

(B)   Tropospheric lightning storms do not actually play a role in Atlantic hurricane formation.

(C)   A reduction in lightning storms in the Ethiopian highlands would not reduce the Atlantic hurricane season.

(D)   More hurricanes would form in the Atlantic if there were no Ethiopian lightning storms.

(E)   If Saharan atmospheric waves could reach the Caribbean, hurricane formation would increase even more in that region.

26. According to recent study data, greenhouse gas emissions from fossil fuel-based vehicles are a major contributor to global climate instability. One plan to reduce greenhouse gases within the United States is to encourage the production of corn-based ethanol fuels. Such "biofuels" burn cleaner, and therefore emit fewer harmful chemicals into the atmosphere. To encourage production, financial incentives could be given to companies that make the switch to biofuel technology.

Which of the following, if true, would cast the most doubt on the effectiveness of the plan to reduce greenhouse gas emissions by encouraging the production of corn-based fuels?

(A) Before any law is enacted to provide financial incentives to biofuel companies, it must pass with a majority vote in both houses of Congress.

(B) While ethanol currently makes up less than 4 percent of the motor fuel used nationally, the corn used in ethanol production constitutes 14 percent of the domestic crop.

(C) Corn-based ethanol production increases food prices and consumes large amounts of water.

(D) The fertilizer used in the cultivation of biofuel crops releases nitrous oxide, a potent, long-lived greenhouse gas, into the atmosphere.

(E) The scientific study on greenhouse gas emissions was conducted by a university that received funding from prominent agricultural lobby groups who would benefit greatly from new legislation.

27. A football team's fans expect the team to make the playoffs. If the team makes the playoffs then their fans expect it to win the Super Bowl. A team that is happy just to make the playoffs will upset its fans. The New York Giants' primary goal is to meet their fans' expectations .

Which of the following must be true based on the statements above?

(A) Other teams will not upset their fans only if they win the Super Bowl.

(B) A team that doesn't think its fans want it to make the playoffs will certainly not make the playoffs.

(C) The Giants' primary goal is possible only if they win the Super Bowl.

(D) If a team is happy just to make the playoffs one year, it won't make the playoffs next year.

(E) The Giants' fans are not currently upset.

28. The Anaheim Aardvarks, a new professional football team, give out free group tickets to sponsors to encourage their continued financial support. However, ticket scalpers have found a way to exploit this practice. Ticket scalpers purchase these tickets outside of the stadium gates and sell them at full price to others due to high demand, causing the Aardvarks to lose revenue.

To discourage the buying and selling of free tickets, it would be best for the Anaheim Aardvarks to:

(A) Restrict the number of free tickets that are given out for any particular event.

(B) Require that people holding free tickets use a special entrance where stadium employees could verify an individual's group affiliation.

(C) Limit the use of the free tickets to only certain games or sporting events.

(D) Restrict the type of free tickets to the less-expensive upper bowl seating.

(E) Discontinue group promotions and free tickets for the most popular games of the season.

29. Pharmaceutical manufacturers have long claimed that one of the main reasons they give doctors free drug samples is so that doctors can pass the medicine along to poor patients. However, a new study shows that high-income, well-insured individuals receive considerably more prescription drug samples than do low-income, poorly insured individuals. This is because doctors favor affluent people with health insurance.

   Which of the following, if true, most seriously jeopardizes the validity of the explanation for why high-income individuals receive more free prescription drug samples than low-income individuals do?

(A) Independent medical clinics not affiliated with large hospitals receive only a small percentage of free drug samples from pharmaceutical manufacturers.

(B) Because of the associated costs, low-income people see doctors less often, if at all.

(C) Some medical offices refuse to treat individuals for conditions that are not critical or life-threatening if the individual does not have the means to pay for the treatment.

(D) Once the free drug sample supply is gone in a doctor's office, the patients are forced to pay for their prescriptions.

(E) Though they claim to give doctors free drug samples in order to help poor patients, the real reasons pharmaceutical companies do it are to increase brand awareness and to influence the doctor to prescribe more of the drugs.

30.   In the early 20th century, ivory poaching led to the near extinction of the black
        rhino and the African elephant. As a result, numerous African nations supported
        a complete ban on all ivory sales. This ban has been in effect since 1989. The
        governments of South Africa, Botswana, and Namibia have recently put up for
        auction thousands of tons of confiscated ivory horns and tusks, in spite of the
        continued moratorium. However, the three governments have the full support
        of the same conservationists who helped impose the 1989 international ban on
        ivory sales.

        Which of the following, if true, contributes most to an explanation of why
        conservationists support South Africa's, Botswana's, and Namibia's auction
        of ivory?

(A)   The international demand for ivory has decreased significantly since 1989.

(B)   Most wild black rhinos and African elephants live outside of South Africa,
        Botswana, and Namibia.

(C)   Once the tons of confiscated ivory are auctioned, the market will be flooded
        with ivory, making poaching economically impractical.

(D)   If it were not for the auction, the confiscated ivory could never be used, and
        would have to remain in government warehouses.

(E)   Due to major conservation efforts, black rhino and African elephant populations
        have slowly but steadily increased in the last few years.

31.   Arbor Day was founded in 1872 to promote the planting and growth of trees in the United States. Proponents of Arbor Day argue that the large-scale planting of trees would be beneficial for the environment. Trees reduce erosion, provide homes for animals, and draw harmful pollutants out of the atmosphere. As a result, they advocate that land should be set aside to plant millions of acres of trees.

Which of the following, if true, most seriously weakens the conclusion drawn by the Arbor Day proponents above?

(A)   2.6 million acres of trees are already planted annually in the United States, without any additional impetus needed.

(B)   Studies have shown that large tree plantations can reduce stream flow, use large amounts of water, and consume essential nutrients in poor soils, leaving the soils salty and acidic.

(C)   When Hurricane Katrina hit the Gulf Coast, it destroyed 320 million trees, resulting in over 424 million tons of carbon dioxide being released into the atmosphere.

(D)   Deforestation has been linked to decreased evapotranspiration, which lessens atmospheric moisture and decreases precipitation downwind from the deforested area.

(E)   The United States has the 7th highest rate of primary forest loss of any country in the world.

32. It is cheaper to buy a plasma television in Delaware, which has no sales tax, than to buy a plasma television in New York City, which has a seven percent sales tax. Even after gas and tolls, it is cheaper for someone in New York City to go to Delaware to buy a plasma television.

Based on the statements above, which of the following must be true?

(A) It is cheaper for the plasma television manufacturer to ship the television to Delaware than to New York City.

(B) If many people who live in New York City buy electronics in Delaware, electronics retailers in New York City will go out of business.

(C) The cost of gas and tolls for a roundtrip from New York City to Delaware is less than seven percent of the cost of a plasma television.

(D) Gas costs at least seven percent less in Delaware than in New York City.

(E) More plasma televisions are sold in Delaware than in New York City.

33.   Recent market research has indicated that, because Globaltech's current line of cell phones has remained the same over the last few years without adding any cutting-edge features that consumers demand, it has lost considerable market share in the industry. So, in an attempt to regain market share, Globaltech has proposed a new line of cell phones with the capability of synchronizing various household appliances such as computers, light switches, and even toasters.

Which of the following, if true, provides the strongest reason to expect that the proposed line of cell phones will be successful in regaining market share?

(A)   Engineers have only recently been able to discover a cost-effective way to remotely control household appliances through cell phones.

(B)   An increasing number of countries throughout the world now have more cell phones than people.

(C)   The number of appliances that can be remotely controlled through a cell phone signal has more than tripled in the last few years.

(D)   Globaltech's market share began decreasing at the same time as it stopped adding new features to its cell phones.

(E)   In today's economy, the new time-saving ability to remotely control appliances is being demanded by more and more consumers.

34. Numerous ancient Mayan cities have been discovered in the Yucatan peninsula in recent decades. The ruins lack any evidence of destruction by invading forces, internal revolts, or disease, and appear simply to have been abandoned. Some archaeologists have theorized that the cities were abandoned due to a severe drought known to have occurred in the region between 800 and 1000 A.D.

Which of the following, if true, most strongly supports the archaeologists' theory?

(A) Ample archaeological evidence of Mayan peasant revolts and city-state warfare exists, but such events could never result in the permanent abandonment of cities.

(B) No monumental inscriptions created after 900 A.D. have been found in these cities, but inscriptions dating before that time have been found in abundance.

(C) Studies of Yucatan lake sediment cores provide conclusive evidence that a prolonged drought occurred in the region from 800 to 1000 A.D.

(D) Climatic studies have documented cycles of intermittent drought in the Yucatan peninsula dating from the present to at least 7,000 years ago.

(E) The Mayan city, Uxmal, was continuously inhabited from 500-1550 A.D.

35. Researchers have recently discovered that approximately 70% of restaurant lemon wedges they studied were contaminated with harmful microorganisms such as bacteria and fungal pathogens. The researchers looked at numerous different restaurants in different regions of the country. Most of the organisms had the potential to cause infectious disease. For that reason, people should not order lemon wedges with their drinks.

Which of the following, if true, would most weaken the conclusion above?

(A) The researchers could not determine why or how the microbial contamination occurred on the lemon wedges.

(B) The researchers failed to investigate contamination of restaurant lime wedges by harmful microorganisms.

(C) The researchers found that people who ordered the lemon wedges at restaurants were equally likely to contract the diseases caused by the discovered bacteria as were people who did not order lemon wedges.

(D) Health laws require lemons to be handled with gloves or tongs, but the common practice for waiters and waitresses is to handle them with their bare hands.

(E) Many factors affect the chance of an individual contracting a disease by coming into contact with bacteria that have nothing to do with lemons. These factors include things such as health and age of the individual, as well as the status of their immune system.

36.   Fearing the possibility of a detrimental surge in steel imports that could cripple the domestic steel industry, the government imposed stiff tariffs on all imported steel in 2002. As a direct result, several industries that depend upon the steel market (such as the automobile, heavy machinery, and shipbuilding industries) faced increased costs, making it more difficult for those industries to compete in their own export markets.

Which of the following can be most properly inferred from the passage?

(A)   Before the tariff, steel had been cheaper to import than it was to purchase domestically.

(B)   The imposed steel tariffs gave a strong boost to domestic steel companies that allowed them to stay in business.

(C)   The automobile, heavy machinery, and shipbuilding industries depend upon export markets for a large percentage of their profits.

(D)   The steel needs of the automobile, heavy machinery, and shipbuilding industries could not be met solely through domestic steel production.

(E)   Before 2002, more steel was imported into the country than was exported.

37.   **Studies show that the percentage of American children who are obese is greater than that of any other nation.** One school of thought attributes this problem to the lack of exercise American children get, citing the absence of required physical education classes in elementary schools. **Another group feels that the array of unhealthy snacks produced for children is to blame.** Clearly, both rationales are equally valid.

The two portions in **boldface** play which of the following roles?

(A)   The first serves as the conclusion of the argument; the second is evidence on which the conclusion is based.

(B)   The first serves as the conclusion of the argument; the second is the point of view that the conclusion opposes.

(C)   The first is a premise for which different potential causes will be presented; the second is one of the potential causes.

(D)   The first is a premise for which different potential causes will be presented; the second is a potential cause that is introduced and rejected.

(E)   The first is evidence for which two conclusions will be drawn; the second is the author's rebuttal of both conclusions.

38. Unlike the wholesale cost of virgin paper pulp from harvested wood, the wholesale price of recycled paper pulp has fallen appreciably in the last few months. Though the retail price of recycled paper products such as copy paper and cardboard boxes has not yet fallen, it will inevitably fall.

Which of the following, if true, most seriously weakens the argument above?

(A) The cost of processing recycled paper pulp into new paper has increased in the last few months.

(B) The wholesale price of virgin paper pulp is generally higher than that of the same amount of recycled paper pulp.

(C) The average operating costs of paper stores and suppliers have remained virtually constant for the last two years.

(D) Due to "price stickiness," retail prices tend to lag behind changes in wholesale prices.

(E) The cost of collecting scrap paper – the raw material used to make recycled paper pulp – has increased in the last year.

39.   During national economic upturns, the demand for luxury items such as high-
        end automobiles or clothing increases, often resulting in substantial increases in
        price. This increase in price is measurable even in regions of the country where
        the economic upturn is not locally felt.

        Which of the following conclusions is best supported by the statement above?

(A)   People buy more luxury items during economic upturns because discretionary
        income is easier to come by.

(B)   National economic upturns have little, if any effect on local prices of luxury items,
        as long as the local demand for those luxury items does not increase.

(C)   The luxury-item market conditions for local areas are connected to the national
        economy, even if local economic trends do not match national averages.

(D)   Regions of the country that have very little demand for luxury items are affected
        less by national economic upturns.

(E)   National economic downturns can cause local decreases in the prices of
        luxury items.

40.   Heavy consumption of alcohol causes impaired judgment, a loss of fine motor skills, slower reaction times, a decrease in visual acuity, and other short-term symptoms. Since alcohol can be metabolized in the average person's body at a rate of 0.015 BAC (or "blood alcohol content") per hour, a severely intoxicated individual with a BAC of 0.15 should be symptom-free after 10 hours. After this time, if the individual exhibits similar symptoms, such symptoms cannot be caused by alcohol.

Which of the following, if true, most seriously weakens the conclusion above?

(A)   Some symptoms normally associated with alcohol consumption may resemble symptoms caused by prescription drugs or even drowsiness.

(B)   Increases in BAC are based off of the amount of alcohol consumed, not the number of drinks (some drinks contain more alcohol than others).

(C)   Heavy alcohol consumption has numerous long-term effects such as cirrhosis of the liver, stomach ulcers, and birth defects.

(D)   The metabolization rate of alcohol varies depending upon a person's health, weight, diet, and genetic predispositions.

(E)   Some people, due to an acute sensitivity to alcohol, cannot even reach a BAC of 0.15 before becoming violently ill.

41.   The demand for quinine, an ancient Peruvian derivative from the cinchona tree used to treat malaria, is slowly diminishing in sub-Saharan Africa. Since quinine is still one of the most cost-effective antimalarial drugs to produce, government officials in sub-Saharan African nations attribute the decrease in demand to their active insecticide campaign against the anopheles mosquito, the primary vector for transmitting the disease.

Which of the following, if true, would most seriously weaken the government officials' explanation for the lower demand for quinine?

(A)   Spraying the interior walls of living structures with insecticide is much more cost-effective than wide-scale field spraying.

(B)   Mosquito nets have been shown to greatly reduce the rate of malarial infection, but only 1 out of 20 people in Africa own a bed net.

(C)   A mutated strain of malaria, resistant to quinine, has spread into Africa from Asia within the last few decades.

(D)   More than 1.7 million people die of malaria every year in Sub-Saharan Africa, comprising almost 90% of all worldwide malaria deaths.

(E)   Massive insecticide spraying against malaria took place in many regions of Africa in the 1950s, with mixed results.

42.   The administrative budget in the Central Valley school district is proportionate to the value of the valley's property tax base, the chief source of funding for the school district. As revenue from property taxes increases, each budget segment of the school district is increased proportionately.

Which of the following statements, if true, is the best basis for a criticism of the Central Valley's budgeting policy as an economically sound budgeting method for school districts?

(A)   The school district might continue to pay for past inefficient allocation of funds.

(B)   The revenue from property taxes has remained relatively unchanged for the last decade.

(C)   Student performance is affected by fluctuations in the overall school district budget.

(D)   Many Central Valley taxpayers have complained about the high property tax rates in the area.

(E)   The current budgeting system has little impact on whether parents decide to take their children to non-district funded classes.

43.   Some of the staff at the local daycare suggest that parents would be better
        incentivized to pick up their children on time if the parents were assessed a fine
        after arriving more than 10 minutes late to pick up their children.

        Which of the following, assuming that it is a realistic possibility, argues most
        strongly against the effectiveness of the suggestion above?

(A)   By replacing social norms with market norms, fines might induce parents to
        weigh the "costs" of picking their children up late and, as a result, to frequently
        choose to be late.

(B)   There might be irreconcilable disagreements among the daycare staff about
        whether the late fines should be imposed.

(C)   Late fines might cause some parents to enroll their children in other daycares.

(D)   Removing the late fine policy might actually increase the number of tardy pick-ups.

(E)   Some parents might pick up their children late no matter what level of fine is
        imposed against them.

44. When Germany was asked to pay 132 billion gold marks in war reparations following World War I, the German government had to print money to pay its bills, drastically devaluing the currency. In response to this anticipated devaluation, Germans began spending their money while it still had purchasing power, almost completely depleting the monetary stores of domestic banks.

Which of the following, if true, taken together with the information above, best supports the conclusion that the devaluation of the German mark was likely to continue?

(A) The recipient governments of the war reparations began to demand that the reparations be paid in goods and commodities, such as coal.

(B) The amount of 132 billion gold marks was the largest war reparations amount ever levied to that point.

(C) In the post-World War I period, the German government had only two options for preventing complete economic collapse: print money or take out loans from domestic banks.

(D) Printing currency causes inflation when the money is not based on hard assets such as gold or land.

(E) The more consumers make purchases, the more money is returned into a country's economy.

45.   Daylight Saving Time (DST) was originally conceived by Benjamin Franklin to reduce the costs associate with artificial lighting such as candles. By shifting the "time" of the summer months to one hour later, studies have shown that DST reduces the yearly cost of lighting and small appliances in a home by approximately 4%. Nevertheless, greater energy savings might be realized without DST. Therefore, Daylight Savings Time should be abandoned completely within the United States.

Which of the following, if true, most strongly supports the claim above about Daylight Savings Time?

(A)   Because of the shift in twilight hours, pedestrians are three times as likely to be hit and killed by cars right after the DST switch.

(B)   Some countries straddle international time zones and therefore have fractional time zones, 30 or 45 minutes ahead of their neighbors.

(C)   Within the United States, DST is already not observed in Arizona and Hawaii, as well as numerous U.S. Territories.

(D)   With the advent of air conditioning devices, the "energy curve" in the summer months means DST causes a net increase in U.S. electricity costs.

(E)   The more DST becomes embedded in technology like computers and media players, the higher the cost will be to change back to a non-DST system.

Challenge Problems

46. The purpose of a general theory of art is to explain every aesthetic feature that is found in any of the arts. Pre-modern general theories of art, however, focused primarily on painting and sculpture. Every pre-modern general theory of art, even those that succeed as theories of painting and sculpture, fails to explain some aesthetic feature of music.

   The statements above, if true, most strongly support which one of the following?

(A) Any general theory of art that explains the aesthetic features of painting also explains those of sculpture.

(B) A general theory of art that explains every aesthetic feature of music will achieve its purpose.

(C) Any theory of art that focuses primarily on sculpture and painting cannot explain every aesthetic feature of music.

(D) No pre-modern general theory of art achieves its purpose unless music is not art.

(E) No pre-modern general theory of art explains any aesthetic features of music that are not shared with painting and sculpture.

47. **Raymond:** Although some people claim it is inconsistent to support freedom of speech and also support legislation limiting the amount of violence in TV programs, it is not. We can limit TV program content because the damage done by violent programs is more harmful than the decrease in freedom of speech that would result from the limitations envisioned by the legislation.

    Which one of the following principles, if valid, most helps to justify Raymond's reasoning?

(A)   In evaluating legislation that would impinge on a basic freedom, we should consider the consequences of not passing the legislation.

(B)   One can support freedom of speech while at the same time recognizing that other interests can sometimes override it.

(C)   When facing a choice between restricting freedom of speech or not, we must decide based on what would make the greatest number of people the happiest.

(D)   If the exercise of a basic freedom leads to some harm, then the exercise of that freedom should be restricted.

(E)   In some circumstances, we should tolerate regulations that impinge on a basic freedom.

48.   A newspaper article in the Smithville Herald argued that the strength of unions was declining. The article's evidence was the decreasing number and size of strikes, as if the reason for the unions' existence was to organize strikes. Surely, in a modern industrial society, the calling of a strike is evidence that the negotiaing position of the union was too weak. Strong unions do not need to call strikes. They can concentrate their efforts on working with others in the labor market to achieve common goals, such as profitable and humane working conditions.

The argument criticizing the newspaper article employs which one of the following strategies?

(A)   Questioning the accuracy of the statistical evidence that the newspaper article uses

(B)   Detailing historical changes that make the newspaper article's analysis outdated

(C)   Reinterpreting evidence that the newspaper article uses as indicating the opposite of what the newspaper concludes

(D)   Arguing that the newspaper article's conclusion is motivated by a desire to change the role of unions

(E)   Pointing to common interests among unions and management

49.   Before 1986 physicists believed they could describe the universe in terms of four universal forces. Experiments then suggested, however, a fifth universal force of mutual repulsion between particles of matter. This fifth force would explain the occurrence in the experiments of a smaller measurement of the gravitational attraction between bodies than the established theory predicted.

Which one of the following, if true, most strengthens the argument that there is a fifth universal force?

(A)   The extremely sophisticated equipment used for the experiments was not available to physicists before the 1970s.

(B)   No previously established scientific results are incompatible with the notion of a fifth universal force.

(C)   Some scientists have suggested that the alleged fifth universal force is an aspect of gravity rather than being fundamental in itself.

(D)   The experiments were conducted by physicists in remote geological settings in which factors affecting the force of gravity could not be measured with any degree of precision.

(E)   The fifth universal force was postulated at a time in which many other exciting and productive ideas in theoretical physics were developed.

50.   **Ravi:** The highest priority should be given to the needs of the sales department, because without successful sales the company as a whole would fail.

Ed: There are several departments other than sales that must also function successfully for the company to succeed. It is impossible to give the highest priority to all of them.

Ed criticizes Ravi's argument by pointing out:

(A)   That the sales department taken by itself is not critical to the company's success as a whole.

(B)   The ambiguity of the term "highest priority".

(C)   That the departments other than sales are more vital to the company's success.

(D)   An absurd consequence of its apparent assumption that a department's necessity earns it the highest priority.

(E)   That Ravi makes a generalization from an atypical case.

51.   Researchers have found that people who drink five or more cups of coffee a day have a risk of heart disease 2.5 times the average after corrections are made for age and smoking habits. Members of the research team say that, on the basis of their findings, they now limit their own daily coffee intake to two cups.

        Which of the following, if true, indicates that the researchers' precaution might NOT have the result of decreasing their risk of heart disease?

(A)   The study found that for people who drank three or more cups of coffee daily, the additional risk of heart disease increased with each extra daily cup.

(B)   Per capita coffee consumption has been declining over the past 20 years because of the increasing popularity of soft drinks and because of health worries.

(C)   The study did not collect information that would show whether variations in the level of coffee consumption are directly related to variations in level of stress, a major causal factor in heart disease.

(D)   Subsequent studies have consistently shown that heavy smokers consume coffee at about 3 times the rate of nonsmokers.

(E)   Subsequent studies have shown that heavy coffee consumption tends to cause an elevated blood-cholesterol level, an immediate indicator of increased risk of heart disease.

52.   People who have political power tend to see new technologies as a means of extending or protecting their power, whereas they generally see new ethical arguments and ideas as a threat to it. Therefore, technical ingenuity usually brings benefits to those who have this ingenuity, whereas ethical inventiveness brings only pain to those who have this inventiveness.

Which one of the following statements, if true, most strengthens the argument?

(A)   Those who offer new ways of justifying current political power often reap the benefits of their own innovations.

(B)   Politically powerful people tend to reward those whom they believe are useful to them and to punish those whom they believe are threats.

(C)   Ethical inventiveness and technical ingenuity are never possessed by the same individuals.

(D)   New technologies are often used by people who strive to defeat those who currently have political power.

(E)   Many people who possess ethical inventiveness conceal their novel ethical arguments for fear of retribution by the politically powerful.

53.   **Alonso:** The introduction of a new drug into the marketplace should be
       contingent upon our having a good understanding of its social impact. However,
       the social impact of the newly marketed antihistamine is far from clear. It is
       obvious, then, that there should be a general reduction in the pace of bringing
       to the marketplace new drugs that are now being created.

       Which one of the following, if true, most strengthens the argument?

(A)   The social impact of the new antihistamine is much better understood than that
       of most new drugs being tested.

(B)   The social impact of some of the new drugs being tested is poorly understood.

(C)   The economic success of some drugs is inversely proportional to how well we
       understand their social impact.

(D)   The new antihistamine is chemically similar to some of the new drugs being tested.

(E)   The new antihistamine should be next on the market only if most new drugs
       being tested should be on the market also.

54. In a recent study, a group of subjects had their normal daily caloric intake increased by 25 percent. This increase was entirely in the form of alcohol. Another group of similar subjects had alcohol replace non-alcoholic sources of 25 percent of their normal daily caloric intake. All subjects gained body fat over the course of the study, and the amount of body fat gained was the same for both groups.

Which one of the following is most strongly supported by the information above?

(A) Alcohol is metabolized more quickly by the body than are other food or drinks.

(B) In the general population, alcohol is the primary cause of gains in body fat.

(C) An increased amount of body fat does not necessarily imply a weight gain.

(D) Body fat gain is not dependent solely on the number of calories one consumes.

(E) The proportion of calories from alcohol in a diet is more significant for body gain than are the total calories from alcohol.

55.   When investigators discovered that the director of a local charity had repeatedly
       overstated the number of people his charity had helped, the director accepted
       responsibility for the deception. However, the investigators claimed that
       journalists were as much to blame as the director was for inflating the
       charity's reputation, since they had naïvely accepted what the director told
       them, and simply reported as fact the numbers he gave them.

       Which one of the following principles, if valid, most helps to justify the
       investigators' claim?

(A)   Anyone who works for a charitable organization is obliged to be completely
       honest about the activities of that organization.

(B)   Anyone who knowingly aids a liar by trying to conceal the truth from others is
       also a liar.

(C)   Anyone who presents as factual a story that turns out to be untrue without first
       attempting to verify that story is no less responsible for the consequences of that
       story than anyone else is.

(D)   Anyone who lies in order to advance his or her own career is more deserving of
       blame than someone who lies in order to promote a good cause.

(E)   Anyone who accepts responsibility for a wrongful act that he or she committed
       is less deserving of blame than someone who tries to conceal his or her own
       wrongdoing.

Solutions

Lesson Solutions

1. (B)

This is, of course, a Strengthen question ("would most strengthen the ... argument"). Dr. Larson argues that sleep deprivation is a problem and concludes ("Therefore") that we "should restructure the workday to allow people flexibility in scheduling." The missing premise is, of course, that a flexible work schedule would allow people to get more sleep. The conclusion dealt with reducing sleep deprivation by allowing scheduling flexibility. (A), (D), and (E): These answers incorrectly focus on the length of the workday rather than the positive impact of scheduling flexibility. (C): This answer is simply irrelevant to the argument. Because this is a Strengthen question, we add a premise with our answer and hence can apply ANT – the assumption negation technique. If we negate the correct answer and say "employees would not get more sleep if they had more scheduling flexibility," this statement would totally undermine the author's conclusion. Applying ANT proves (B) is the correct answer.

2. (A)

This is a Weaken question ("most calls into question"). (A): This answer provides a plausible alternative explanation: even if the nutrients of juice and un-juiced fruits and vegetables are the same, people might be more likely to consume those nutrients in liquid form. Thus, home juicers do provide a unique property. (B): This answer supports (not weakens) Nate's conclusion. (C): This answer does not address the primary conclusion about nutrition. (D) and (E): These answers are not truly relevant, but support Nate's argument.

3. (C)

This is an Inference question since "the information above ... supports ... the following." Note that when the question stem calls for information in the stimulus to support the correct answer choice (as it does here), that answer choice will be a conclusion/inference. When the question stem calls for the answer choice to support the stimulus, you are seeking a premise (Strengthen). The limited scope of the premises should help you select the correct answer. "Most antidepressant drugs cause weight gain." "... some weight gain is unlikely to be preventable." Since this is an Inference question, the correct answer must be true. (A) and (B): These answers are incorrect since they are not necessarily true (for example, what if the patient is suicidal?). Also, the universal statements (such as "should not prescribe" in choice A) are inconsistent with the scope of the premises. (D): This answer is incorrect since it contradicts a premise ("While dieting can help reduce the amount of weight gained"). The universal statement "should be attributed" is inconsistent with

the careful scope of the premises. (E): This answer is incorrect since it is not necessarily true. The universal statement "should diet" is inconsistent with the careful scope of the premises.

4. **(A)**
This is a Method problem ("which of the following argumentative techniques"). (A): This answer correctly describes Weber's argumentative technique. Imran states a general proposition, Weber responds with a specific counterexample. (B): This answer is incorrect since Weber does not explain a phenomenon. (C): This answer is incorrect since Weber does not make an analogy (which would include "like"). (D): This answer is incorrect since Weber does not comment on any ambiguity. (E): This answer is incorrect since Weber does not exclude any alternatives.

5. **(D)**
This is a Mimic the Reasoning question ("most parallel, in its logical structure"). Careful reading is the secret to solving Mimic the Reasoning questions. (A): This answer describes a cold place, then uses an example of a warm environment, so the test-taker should eliminate it. (B) and (C): These answers both begin in the positive ("It is accurate" and "It is correct"), so the test-taker should eliminate them immediately. (D): This answer, like the stimulus, shows that something can be an indirect cause. (E): This answer does not describe an indirect cause, rather, it describes a relationship separated by one degree – choice (E) is close, but inferior to (D).

6. **(D)**
This is an Explain question ("resolve the apparent discrepancy"). The correct answer must explain the paradox of why removing lead paint would actually lead to more ingestion. (D): This answer does that nicely, removal would lead to dust and dust is easier to ingest than paint on the walls. (A): This answer is incorrect because it does not resolve the discrepancy about the removal of lead paint (any information about lead-free paint is irrelevant). (B): This answer is incorrect. The monetary impact is irrelevant to resolving the discrepancy. (C): This answer is incorrect because it does not resolve the discrepancy. Even if it is true that other sources are responsible for most of the lead, the paradox is why paint removal would lead to more lead ingestion, rather than less. (E): This answer is incorrect. Other environmental hazards are irrelevant to resolving the discrepancy.

7. **(B)**
This is a Roles question. The correct answer describes the function of the two bolded statements within the argument. (B): This answer accurately describes the roles of the two bolded statements. The first is a statement of the analysts' position; the second defines the difference of opinion. (A): This answer is incorrect. The first statement is not evidence, but a position, and the second is not a position. (C): This answer is incorrect. The second portion is not evidence in support of the first. (D): This answer is incorrect. The first statement is not evidence, and the second statement does not support an opposed position. (E): This answer is incorrect. The second portion is not a position but a description of the disagreement.

Assorted Problem Solutions

8. (C)

The question asks the reader to strengthen the conclusion that *The Office* was only widely watched because of its timeslot, following *My Name is Earl*, and not because of the show itself. (A) and (E): These answers are out of scope, providing new information but not touching on the conclusion itself. (D): This answer also leans toward weakening the conclusion by rationalizing away the recent poor performance of the show, noting that it is currently facing greater competition. (C): This answer is the correct answer, as it demonstrates that the timeslot is successful with another show, which helps to strengthen the idea that the timeslot itself is what makes the show popular.

9. (B)

This is an Explain question. The paradox is how raisins could have more iron per food calorie. (B):This answer provides the only logical explanation. If B is true, raisins and grapes would have the same amount of iron, but raisins would actually have fewer food calories. Thus, raisins would contain more iron per food calorie. (A): This answer, a very popular choice, is incorrect since it only addresses the volume of the portions; iron-per-calorie could still be exactly the same. (C), (D), and (E): These answers do not address the issue of iron per calorie, and therefore are incorrect.

10. (D)

This Roles question asks us to consider how the argument is structured, specifically the two boldfaced parts. To do this we must understand the author's main point: that libraries are worthy of public funding because books are great pleasures. The first boldfaced statement presents the opposing point of view: libraries should not be publicly funded. The second boldfaced statement presents the author's viewpoint. Thus, the correct answer is D.

11. (C)

This is an Explain question. When comets break up they emit gas and dust; gas and dust lead to increased brightness. The paradox: how were the astronomers able to detect the brightness before the comet broke up? (C): This answer provides a reasonable explanation, as gas and dust could have been emitted just before the comet disintegrated. (A): This answer is incorrect since the comet would not be brighter (and hence visible) if it were not emitting gas and dust. (B): This answer is incorrect. While this answer explains why a disintegrating comet is brighter, it does not help resolve the paradox of why the Steinman-Arnett 3 comet was brighter before it was visibly breaking up. (D): This answer does not resolve why the comet was 1,000 times brighter in September, but observations revealed no pieces until November. (E): This answer is incorrect. This answer may explain why the comet broke up, but does not help resolve the paradox.

12. (D)

This is a Strengthen question ("justify"). The author concludes that one "should not always purchase technologically advanced educational tools" – but why? The evidence the

author presents shows that low tech tools were no worse than high tech, not necessarily better. Thus, the author must have an additional reason. (D): This answer calls for similar results and less cost. It supports the author's conclusion by providing the missing premise. (A): This answer is incorrect since it focuses on an aspect (military vs. civilian) that is not part of the conclusion. (B): This answer is incorrect since it may explain but does not support the author's conclusion. (C): This answer is not consistent with or relevant to the author's argument. (E): This answer is incorrect since it contradicts the author's conclusion. The scope of this answer ("should always") is inconsistent with the scope of the stimulus.

13. **(A)**
This is a Weaken question. (A): This answer undermines the conclusion by noting the importance of understanding principles. (B): This answer is incorrect since it does not undermine the conclusion. (C) and (D): These answers are incorrect since they actually support the conclusion. (E): This answer is incorrect since it does not undermine the conclusion about less emphasis on mathematical principles.

14. **(B)**
This is a Strengthen question. The conclusion is that peat harvesting in this country would not threaten the ecological balance since the water supply in Ireland has not been contaminated by centuries of peat harvesting. (A): This answer is irrelevant since it does not deal with peat harvesting. (B): This answer strengthens the argument by indicating that the results in Ireland are applicable in this country (since the original ecology was "virtually identical"). (C): This answer is irrelevant since it does not deal with peat harvesting. (D): This answer is irrelevant since it does not mention anything about the effect on the ecology. (E): This answer is irrelevant since it does not mention anything about the effect on the ecology.

15. **(D)**
This is a Method of Reasoning question, which becomes clear after reading the answer choices. The correct answer choice must accurately describe the argumentative technique used by the drilling proponent. (A): This answer is incorrect since the proponent offers no evidence. (B): This answer is incorrect since the proponent does not contradict any statistics. (C): This answer is incorrect since the proponent does not point out a misapplication of an argumentative technique. (D): This answer correctly describes the argumentative approach followed by the proponent: citing a parallel argument ("might just as well argue …"). The drilling proponent completely ignores the issue of risk, instead choosing to focus exclusively on the other half of the opponent's argument: that new drilling should not be allowed because so little total oil is produced. The proponent compares that to prohibiting new farms because they add so little to the total amount of food produced – a strikingly unsupported notion. (E): This answer is incorrect since the proponent does not propose a conclusion.

16. **(B)**
This is a Roles question. It asks us to consider how the argument is structured, specifically the two boldfaced parts. To do this we must understand the author's main point: Alexis must be accepted into a top MBA program because she fulfills two necessary require-

ments. The first bolded statement presents the two necessary conditions. The second bolded statement is the argument's conclusion. However, the necessary conditions presented may not be sufficient for Alexis to gain entrance to a top program. For example, she may also need a strong undergraduate transcript or glowing letters of recommendation. Regardless, we have no way of knowing whether these two necessary conditions can be treated as sufficient, so the conclusion is not necessarily true and answer (B) is correct.

17. **(B)**
This is an Inference question ("Which of the following conclusions"). (A): The passage does not address the cost of no-till agriculture. (C): The passage does not talk about other agricultural industries. (D): Though the first part of this answer is tempting because the given fraction complements the percentage given in the stimulus, the second part falls outside the scope (demand is never discussed). (E): This answer contains new information that cannot be concluded from the passage. The correct answer is (B).

18. **(E)**
This is a Weaken question ("best criticism of…strategy"). (E): This answer is correct. If (E) is true, than the environmental goals set by the Chinese government would have minimal effect. (E) points out that other national goals would undermine the effectiveness of China's environmental plan. (A): This answer is incorrect because it does not specifically cast doubt on the plan's ability to minimize acid rain. The answer focuses on other forms of air pollution not expressly stated in the original argument. (B): This answer focuses on variations in the effectiveness of the plan, but does not address the overall ability of the plan to reduce acid rain. Therefore, (B) is incorrect. (C): This answer is also incorrect; while it suggests that the goals create unnecessary changes, it does not suggest that the goals will not achieve their purpose. (D): This answer suggests alternative explanations for acid rain, but does not cast doubt on the effectiveness of China's plan to control the factors it has power to control; thus, (D) is incorrect.

19. **(C)**
This is an Explain question ("most helps to explain"). Since the unit labor cost is defined as the average labor cost to manufacture one item in the country, an increase in the hourly compensation rate would have to be offset by an increased rate of making units (i.e., getting paid more to make units faster means the labor cost per unit remains the same.) (C): This answer matches with this idea. (A): This answer is incorrect, because it focuses on the purchase price of the goods, something not mentioned in the passage; purchase price is unrelated to the ratio of labor cost to units produced. (B): This answer provides background information without any linkage between the hourly labor costs and the unit labor costs; raw material costs are unlinked to the ratio of labor costs to units produced. Raw material costs are not included in either statistic. (D): This answer is completely extraneous. (E): This answer, while possibly leading to an increase in productivity, does not explicitly say so. Workers with greater skill levels do not necessarily work faster.

20. **(E)**
This is a Weaken question ("seriously weakens the argument above…"). (E): In this answer, the job of amateur astronomers would become largely ineffectual without the help

of larger, professional telescopes. (E) shows that larger telescopes are essential to the discovery and tracking of NEOs, therefore it is the correct answer. (A): This answer actually strengthens the argument by showing amateur astronomers are more efficient. (B): This answer is wrong because it concentrates on who controls the telescopes, not how the telescopes are controlled, which is the focus of the question. (C): This answer is entirely irrelevant. Just because amateur astronomers have no professional training does not mean they cannot accurately pinpoint NEO orbits. (D): This answer does not contain any information that would weaken the argument, so it is also incorrect

21. **(A)**
This is a Strengthen Question ("would most strengthen the conclusion"). The passage's statistical data support the conclusion, but give information about one year only and identify no factor that would cause a higher long-term accident rate on Highway 105. By describing such a factor (A), the correct answer, suggests that these data can support a generalization like the conclusion. (B): Highway 105's increased patrol officers may simply be an administrative choice and does not indicate a necessary difference in safety. (C): The comparison between the two hospitals also falls apart, because the hospitals likely serve much greater areas than just the two highways alone. (D): This answer weakens the argument by stating that Highway 24 is actually more lethal than Highway 105. (E): This answer contains irrelevant information. We have no way of knowing what impact, if any, the type of asphalt used has on the roads' safety.

22. **(D)**
This is an Inference question ("following conclusions is best supported"). From 1994 to 2001, the violent crime rate in New York City never fell below 851 violent crimes per 100,000 people and never would have exceeded about 700 in the United States. (D): This answer is correct. (Remember that percentage decreases are not equivalent to actual levels.) (A): This answer is not necessarily correct, because even though a lower crime rate in New York City would cause the crime rate in the United States to be lower than it other-wise would, the total crime rate in the United States could still increase due to increases in other regions or cities. Since the problem does not contain any information about law enforcement spending or national effectiveness of law enforcement procedures, (B) and (C) contain new information. Therefore, they cannot be inferred from the passage. (E): This answer extrapolates into the future using current data (something that obviously goes beyond the scope of the question.) It would only be true if current trends continued, which is not something explicitly justifiable from the passage. Therefore, (E) is incorrect.

23. **(A)**
This is a Weaken question ("which of the following…casts the most doubt"). (A): This answer shows that there could be cultural causes unrelated to marketing that may be keeping the substitute from gaining market share across Europe, and therefore weakens the argument. (A) is the correct answer. (B): This answer focuses on the decreasing total size of the yellow fats market, while market share could still proportionally increase. Also, since the product is technically a butter substitute (and thus not butter), it may be immune from the market forces that are causing the butter market to shrink. (C): This

answer provides financial background, but does not undermine the link between the marketing campaign and increase in market share. (D): This answer strengthens, rather than weakens, the argument. (E): This answer is irrelevant. Showing an increase in market share without marketing in one location doesn't mean marketing can't help in another.

24. (B)

This is a Weaken question ("weakens the argument"). This demonstrates a classic logical fallacy with many scientific studies. There is a considerable difference between the statement, "If I regularly consume sugar, I will have a higher risk of pancreatic cancer," and "If I am a person who regularly consumes sugar, I am a person who has a higher risk of pancreatic cancer." The sugar may not actually be the cause. The cause of the cancer could be something else that is correlationally-linked to people that consume sugar. (B): This answer shows this logical fallacy, by indicating an alternative explanation for the cause of the cancer. Therefore, (B) is correct. (A): This answer goes outside of the scope of the question when it talks about other types of cancer; thus (A) is incorrect. (C): This answer may be tempting, since it seems to impy that regular soda drinkers also cnsumer sugar in other parts of their diet. However, this choice does not damage the belief that sugar causes the cancer, and therefore does not weaken the reasoning in favor of diet drinks. (D) and (E): These answers are likewise all extraneous to the argument. (B): This is the only answer that undermines the link between diet drinks and cancer.

25. (A)

This is an Inference question ("draws the most reliable conclusion"). If the Ethiopian lightning storms were the only factor that affected hurricane formation, there would be a difference in the amount of hurricane formation between areas that are affected by the storms and areas that are not. According to the passage, there are regions of hurricane formation that are even more active than the Atlantic seaboard, so Ethiopian lightning storms cannot be the only factor. Therefore, (A) is correct. (B): This answer directly contradicts the passage without any valid grounds. (C), (D), and (E): These answers contain additional information not explicitly supported by the passage; therefore, we cannot determine their validity.

26. (D)

This is a Weaken question ("cast the most doubt"). The focus of the plan is to reduce greenhouse gas emissions within the United States. (D): This answer, by showing that the plan may actually increase greenhouse gas emissions, shows that the plan may not be effective. (D) is therefore correct. (A) and (B): These answers provide background information on the problem, but do not address the focus of the plan. Reducing greenhouse gas emissions. (C): This answer is likewise incorrect. While (C) shows potential negative side effects, the question stem specifically asks us to evaluate the "effectiveness of the plan to reduce greenhouse gas emissions." (C) does not talk about this. (E): This answer tries to cast doubt on the motives of the people doing the study. However, it would be a logical jump outside of the text of the original question to infer that the study was therefore flawed.

27. (C)

This is an Inference question. The Giants' goal is to not upset their fans. Since just making

the playoffs would upset their fans, the Giants, as answer (C) states, must win the Super Bowl. (A): This answer is incorrect since winning the Super Bowl is not the only way to keep from upsetting a team's fans. (B): This answer is incorrect because what a team thinks is irrelevant to this passage. (D): This answer is incorrect since what happens from one year to another is not important to the passage. (E): This answer is incorrect since outside knowledge cannot be used and the passage states nothing about any Giants' success.

28. (B)

This is a Weaken question, albeit a "situational" Weaken question that asks you to make a purpose less likely to be fulfilled ("discourage the buying and selling…"). Requiring verification of an individual's group affiliation would make the tickets valueless for anyone else, so scalping the tickets would no longer be possible. The tickets, however, would still allow the original recipients to enjoy the sporting event. Therefore, (B) is correct. (A): This answer would limit the number of tickets, but it would not discourage the buying and selling of the remaining tickets, nor affect their resale value. (C) and (D): These answers not only fail to prevent scalping, they potentially reduce the usefulness of the tickets. (E): This answer would definitely stop the scalping, but it would also stop the Aardvarks from using the tickets as a promotion.

29. (B)

This is a Weaken question ("most seriously jeopardizes the validity of the explanation"). An alternate explanation of the phenomenon would certainly jeopardize the explanation. (B): This answer, which shows that that low-income people do not see their personal physicans as often (and therefore do not have the opportunity to receive free samples), gives an alternate explanation, and is therefore the correct answer. (A): This answer cannot be correct because it doesn't link back to the original problem (independent medical clinics and large hospitals have nothing to do with it.) (C): This answer actually strengthens the argument by showing that there is a bias toward high-income patients. (D): Even though this answer shows what happens when the free drug samples are depleted, it does not weaken the actual argument. (E): This answer casts doubt on the motives of the pharmaceutical company, but does not jeopardize the validity of the explanation for why high-income individuals receive more free samples than low-income individuals. It might be selected by someone who is not focusing closely enough on what the question is actually asking.

30. (C)

This is an Explain question ("contributes most to an explanation"). The paradox lies in the conservationists' support for the auction of thousands of tons of ivory, when they otherwise supported a total ban on ivory sales. (C): This answer, which shows that the auction would actually help the conservationists' goals, resolves the paradox and is the correct answer. All the other answers focus on background information that is either irrelevant or extraneous. (A), (B), (D), and (E): These answers do not do anything to link the two sides of the paradox together.

31. (B)

This is a Weaken question ("most seriously weakens the conclusion"). The conclusion that land should be set aside to plant millions of acres of trees is based on the argument that large-scale planting is incredibly beneficial for the environment. This would be weakened if evidence shows that there are possible negative ecological consequences for such an action. (B): This answer, which gives such evidence, is the correct answer. (A): This answer suggests that trees are being planted in the United States, but does not weaken the argument to plant more. (C): This answer indicates there are potential negative ecological consequences for forests, but then mentions a completely unrelated cause of those negative consequences. (D): This answer actually strengthens the argument by giving another reason to plant trees. (E): This answer likewise strengthens the argument, showing the United States' relative global ranking in terms of primary forest loss.

32. **(C)**
This is an Inference Question, so the correct answer must be true based on the stimulus. If the TV is cheaper in Delaware even with gas and tolls then it can be logically inferred that those gas and tolls are less than seven percent of the cost of the TV (the amount of sales tax in NYC). This is stated by answer (C). The shipping costs are irrelevant to this passage so (A) can be eliminated. (B): This answer may be true but it too is not relevant to the passage. The difference in gas prices is irrelevant to the passage and cannot be inferred. (E): This answer seems reasonable based on the passage but is not necessarily true.

33. **(E)**
This is a Strengthen question ("strongest reason"). For the proposed line of cell phones to have a chance to attract consumers, the cell phones must have not only cutting-edge features, but also features that consumers demand. (E): This answer provides evidence that this is so, and thus is correct. (A): This answer indicates that the technology is new, but does not say whether consumers demand it. (C): This answer also does not indicate whether consumers want the remote functionality. (B): This answer is completely irrelevant background information. (D): This answer simply reinforces one of the original premises in the argument: that Globaltech has lost market share. It contains no information that would strengthen the original argument.

34. **(B)**
This is a Strengthen question ("which of the following…most strongly supports"). The archaeologists' theory was that the Mayan cities were abandoned due to a severe drought between 800 and 1000 A.D. (B): This answer provides links the abandonment of the cities with the time of the drought, since it supports the archaeologists' theory. (A): This answer, while discounting alternative explanations for the abandonment, does not show anything new. The argument already said there was lack of evidence for those alternative explanations. (C): This answer has a similar flaw. (C) simply repeats information already known in the passage without necessarily strengthening the argument. (D): This answer indicates that droughts exist in the area, but comes no closer to proving the link between the droughts and the abandoned cities. (E): This answer, by showing continual habitation of a Mayan city through that period, weakens the argument.

35. **(C)**
This is a Weaken question ("weaken the conclusion above"). The key phrase in the

conclusion is the word "should" – it implies a value judgment made using certain criteria. Note that the criteria are not mentioned in the passage, therefore, the choice that implies valid criteria and then shows why they are actually irrelevant is the correct answer. (C): This answer does so, by showing that there is no increase in the incidence of infection due to the lemon wedges. This undermines the conclusion. (A): This answer says that the researchers don't know why the contamination occurs, but it doesn't matter why; it only matters that it does. (B), (D), and (E): These answers all provide irrelevant background information that does not weaken the conclusion in any way .

36. **(A)**
This is an Inference question ("most properly inferred"). When the government imposed stiff tariffs on imported steel, the cost of steel rose, so the steel must have been cheaper to import than it was to purchase domestically. Therefore, (A) is correct. All of the other choices contain additional information that cannot be inferred from the passage. (B): We do not know whether the tariffs allowed domestic steel companies to stay in business. (C): We do not know whether certain steel-dependent industries heavily relied on exports. We only know that the tariffs made it more difficult for the steel-dependent companies to compete internationally. (D): There is nothing in the passage about the ability of domestic steel companies to provide for all national needs. (E): There was no mention of an import/export ratio.

37. **(C)**
This is a Roles question that asks us to consider how the argument is structured, specifically the two boldfaced parts. To do this we must understand the purpose of the argument. This argument presents the results of studies and then two alternative causes for the findings, which the author finds equally compelling. The first boldface statement presents the findings of the studies. The second boldface statement is one of the causes. Thus, answer (C) is correct.

38. **(A)**
This is a Weaken question ("weakens the argument"). The argument concludes that declining wholesale prices for recycled pulp will result in declining retail prices. However, there is nothing that says retail prices must decrease because wholesale prices decrease. All things being equal, if wholesale prices decrease, the retailer could choose to pass on the savings to the customer. If, however, other costs associated with the production or sale of a retail product increase, there would be no savings to pass on. (A): This answer shows this possibility and is the correct answer. (B): This answer is irrelevant, since the conclusion has nothing to do with non-recycled products made from virgin paper pulp. (C): This answer indicates that operating costs have remained constant, but "constants" don't change prices! (D): This answer actually strengthens the argument by stating that the price of retail prices will eventually fall. (E): This answer mentions that certain costs in the recycling process have gone up – however, collecting the scrap paper comes before turning it into paper pulp, and therefore would not have any influence on retail price once the wholesale price has been determined.

39. **(C)**

This is an Inference question ("which of the following conclusions"). If the luxury-item markets in local regions were independent of the national economy, fluctuations in the national luxury-item market would not have an effect on local pricing. However, if the statement about national economic upturns is true, it is evidence that local luxury-item markets are connected to the national economy. Therefore, choice (C) is correct. (A): This answer adds additional information explaining why economic upturns cause increases in luxury item prices. However, this explanation cannot be inferred from the original passage. (B): This answer contradicts the claim that national economic upturns affect local luxury item prices, and therefore cannot be true. (D): This answer contains additional information about local luxury item markets that cannot be inferred from the passage. (E): This answer, which talks about economic downturns, contains new information also not inferable from the passage. Just because upturns cause increases in prices does not mean downturns cause decreases.

40. **(D)**

This is a Weaken question ("most seriously weakens"). The passage concludes that, because the average person can metabolize alcohol at a rate of 0.015 BAC per hour, any short-term symptoms normally associated with alcohol could not be caused by alcohol if a person with a BAC of 0.15 is sober for 10 hours. However, according to choice (D), there are factors which could allow alcohol to remain in the bloodstream for longer than normal. Therefore, choice (D) weakens the conclusion and is correct. (A): In this answer the resemblance between alcohol-related symptoms and those caused by other factors is irrelevant. (B): In this answer how many drinks it took for a person to reach a certain BAC level was also irrelevant. (C): The existence of long-term effects of alcohol is not relevant either. (E): The possibility of some people never being able to reach a BAC of 0.15 (choice E) is irrelevant to this issue of whether the individual mentioned in the passage could still have alcohol-related symptoms, as well.

41. **(C)**

This is a Weaken question ("most seriously weaken"). The government officials' explanation assumes that the decrease in the demand for quinine accurately reflects a decrease in the need for quinine – i.e., a decrease in the prevalence of malaria. (C): By giving an alternative explanation for this phenomenon – that quinine is no longer wanted because it is no longer useful against malaria – (C) undermines the officials' explanation and is the correct answer. (A): This answer compares the effectiveness of different methods of insecticide use, which the argument does address. The insecticide program mentioned in the problem could have utilized either (or both) of the methods mentioned. (B): This answer undermines an alternative explanation for the decrease in quinine demand, thus strengthening the argument instead of weakening it. (D): This answer gives background, but does not say whether the insecticide campaign was effective. Theoretically, there could have been a lot more people that died before the supposed campaign. (E): This answer indicates that insecticide spraying has not been effective in the past, but that does not mean it could not be in the future.

42. **(A)**
This is a Weaken question ("the best basis for a criticism"). Notice that the "conclusion" in this argument is actually embedded in the question stem: "Central Valley's budgeting policy is an economically sound budgeting method for school districts." If the original budget incorporated inefficient use of funds, then, since the budgeting policy merely adds to the original budget, these inefficiencies would be preserved. The current policy may therefore not be economically sound, and (A) is correct. (B): This answer implies that the district's budget will not change much, but says nothing about the economic soundness of that budget. (C): This answer shows that the budget has an impact on students, but gives us no basis for evaluating the budgeting method's economic soundness. (D): This answer also offers no grounds for questioning the economic soundness of the budgeting policy, since the school district is not in charge of property tax rates. (E): This answer says that the current budgeting system has little impact on the parents' decision, since it can't be criticized on that basis. Furthermore, (E) is irrelevant as non-district funded classes have nothing to do with the school district's budget.

43. **(A)**
This is a Weaken question ("argues most strongly against"). If assessing fines against late parents actually increased tardiness, this would definitely show the suggestion was not an effective idea. (A): This answer suggests that such a scenario might result from the proposed policy and is thus correct. (B): This answer indicates potential staff disagreements about the late fines, but does not suggest whether or not the late fines would be effective. (C): This answer shows negative consequences for the daycare (decreased enrollment), but still does not evaluate the effectiveness of the proposed late policy. (D): This answer, while it does show a potential increase in tardiness, it is dependent upon removing the policy later on, something which is outside of the scope of the question. (E): This answer is equally irrelevant. Even though some parents might not be affected by the policy, it does not indicate that, as a whole, the parents would not be better motivated.

44. **(C)**
This is a Strengthen question ("best supports the conclusion"). According to the passage, printing money devalued currency, which in turn, led to Germans depleting their savings, which led to a depletion of monetary stores. (C): If this answer is correct, Germany had only two options for immediate financial relief: print money or take out loans from banks. Since the banks' monetary stores were depleted (as per the passage), (C) states that they had to print currency. This, however, would lead to the continuation of the vicious cycle. (A), (B), and (E): These answers simply give background information behind the problem. How the payments were to be made, the total amount of war reparations, and what happens to consumers' money after they spend it are all extraneous to the vicious cycle. (D): This answer states that inflation is caused when money is not backed by hard assets, but there is no information in the passage stating that Germany could not back their currency.

45. **(D)**
This is a Strengthen question ("most strongly supports the claim above"). The original argument is a financial one: the author argues that DST should be abandoned because the

energy costs would be lower. However, the argument does not give any financial evidence of this. (D): This answer, which states that because of air conditioning U.S. energy costs are actually increased due to DST, fills that hole. (A): This answer, while supporting the abandonment of DST, has nothing to do with the original financial-based argument. (B) and (C): In these answers other countries' DST practices and the exceptions to DST within the United States are equally outside the scope of the question. (E): This answer argues that the cost of changing to a non-DST system is becoming increasingly higher, but this has nothing to do with energy savings.

Challenge Solutions

46. (D)

This is an Inference question (the statements in the stimulus serve as premises; the correct answer choice will serve as the conclusion). Only answer (D) must be true, the other answer choices are not necessarily true. (C): This answer is a trap. It is wrong because it states definitively that any theory of art cannot explain every feature of music. Choice C is not necessarily true; the failure described has only been proven for pre-modern general theories, not all theories. (D): This answer, on the other hand, is perfect. We know from the stimulus that the purpose of a general theory of art is to explain every aesthetic feature of a particular kind of art, and no pre-modern general theory explains each of the aesthetic features of music. Thus if music is art, no pre-modern general theory of art has achieved its purpose.

47. (B)

This is a Strengthen question ("helps to justify ... reasoning"). The key to selecting the correct answer choice is to understand the conclusion's scope. Raymond contends that it is not inconsistent to allow one right to trump another. (A): This answer considers the consequences of not passing legislation, which Raymond never discusses. (C): This answer, with the statement "must decide based on ...," is inconsistent with the scope of Raymond's conclusion "can limit" (in this instance, given these considerations). (D): This answer, the most popular wrong answer, goes beyond what Raymond contends. He never states that if a freedom leads to any harm it must be restricted; rather, he merely states that in this particular instance the harm done from violent TV should supercede the modest impingement on one's right to free speech. (E): This answer is inconsistent with the scope of the conclusion since it applies to any "basic freedom," not just freedom of speech.

48. (C)

This is a Method of Reasoning question ("employs which ... of the following strategies"). (C): This answer, the correct answer, accurately describes the criticism as reinterpreting evidence. (A): This answer is incorrect since the stimulus does not question statistical evidence. (B): This answer is incorrect since the stimulus does not detail historical changes to rebut the newspaper article. (D): This answer is incorrect since the stimulus makes no

mention of the motivations for the newspaper article. (E): This answer is incorrect since the stimulus implies common interests with "others in the labor market," not with management.

49. **(B)**
This is a Strengthen question ("strengthens the argument that there is a fifth universal force"). (B): This answer clearly helps. If the notion of a fifth universal element is compatible with previously established scientific results, the conclusion is strengthened. Canceling the double negative may make the statement easier to understand (instead of "No … results are incompatible," restate as "Results … are compatible"). (B): If this answer is negated ("results are not compatible"), the statement would undermine the conclusion. Negating any of the other answers results in a statement that does not undermine the conclusion. Applying the Assumption Negation Technique proves that answer (B) is correct.

50. **(D)**
This is a Method of Reasoning question ("criticizes … by pointing out"). (D): This answer, the correct answer, accurately describes the logic presented in Ed's reply. (A): This answer is a very popular choice, but is wrong. Ed never contends that the sales department is not vitally important; rather he contends that there are other departments that are also critical, and so it would be foolish to give priority to a department on that basis. (B): This answer is incorrect since Ed does not indicate ambiguity about "highest priority." (C): This answer is incorrect since Ed states that other departments "must function successfully," not that those departments are more vital than sales. (E): This answer is incorrect since Ed does not describe Ravi as generalizing from an atypical case.

51. **(C)**
The correct answer choice will indicate that researchers' precautions might not work, so this is a Weaken question. (C): This answer, the correct answer, provides an alternate cause for heart disease. (A) and (B): This answer are incorrect since they do not present evidence that shows the precaution may not have the desired result. (D): This answer is incorrect since the researchers noted that they corrected for smoking habits. (E): This answer is incorrect since it may provide an explanation for how coffee consumption causes heart disease, but does not present evidence that indicates the precaution may not help.

52. **(B)**
This is a Strengthen question. The conclusion is: "Therefore, technical ingenuity usually brings benefits to those who have this ingenuity, whereas ethical inventiveness brings only pain to those who have this inventiveness." (B): This answer matches up perfectly by providing a premise that shows benefits and pain doled out to those identified in the stimulus. (C): This answer is problematic because even if it is true it does nothing to strengthen the conclusion. Applying the Assumption Negation Technique proves that (B) is the correct answer: if answer B were not true, it would undermine the conclusion, but the reverse of other answers would not.

53. **(A)**
This is a Strengthen question ("most strengthens the argument"). The conclusion which

we must strengthen is that there should be a general reduction in the pace of the market introductions of new drugs. (A): This answer strengthens this conclusion because it makes sense to reduce the pace of bringing the new drugs to market if we know less about most of them than the antihistamine. (B): This answer is frequently chosen, but incorrect because it fails to strengthen the conclusion. (B) states that the social impact of some of the new drugs being tested is poorly understood. This wording leaves open the possibility that the social impact of many of the drugs might be well known, failing to strengthen the conclusion, which calls for a general reduction. (C): This answer is also inconsistent with the scope of the conclusion since it mentions "some drugs," and introduces a new topic ("economic success"). (D): This answer is irrelevant since chemical similarity is unrelated to social impact. (E): This answer is inconsistent with the stimulus since the antihistamine is "newly marketed."

54. (D)

This is an Inference question (the statements above are premises, the answer choice is a conclusion "supported by the information above"). (D): This answer must be true – the second group did not increase their caloric intake, yet they gained body fat. (E): This answer may be true, but is not necessarily true. (A): This answer is not supported. The stimulus does not mention any relation between the rate at which food is metabolized and body fat. The topic of this choice is outside the scope of the stimulus. (B): This answer is not supported. The stimulus deals with a group of subjects, not the general population. This conclusion is inconsistent with the scope of the premises. (C): This answer is not supported. The stimulus does not mention weight gain. This conclusion is inconsistent with the scope of the stimulus.

55. (C)

This is a Strengthen question ("justify"). The investigators' claim is that journalists were as much to blame as the director was for inflating the charity's reputation. (C): This answer lays responsibility on those who present a story without verifying it. If this statement were negated, the investigators' claim would be undermined, so choice (C) is the correct answer. (A): This answer is incorrect since it undermines the conclusion. (B): This answer is incorrect because it is irrelevant: the journalists were not accused of knowingly aiding a liar. (D): This answer is incorrect because it, too, is irrelevant. The stimulus did not indicate anyone lied in order to advance his or her career. (E): This answer is incorrect because it is irrelevant to the conclusion about the journalists.

Answer Key

Lesson	Drill	Assorted	Challenge
1 .... B	1 .... S	8 C	46 ...... D
2 .... A	2 I	9 .... B	47 ...... B
3 C	3 ...... E	10 ...... D	48 C
4 ...... A	4 .... S	11 C	49 ...... B
5 ...... D	5 I	12 ...... D	50 ...... D
6 ...... D	6 I	13 ...... A	51 C
7 ...... B	7 I	14 ...... B	52 ...... B
	8 ...... S	15 ...... D	53 ...... A
	9 ...... Method	16 ...... B	54 ...... D
	10 ...... W	17 ...... B	55 C
	11 ...... Mimic	18 ...... E	
	12 ...... Mimic	19 C	
	13 ...... W	20 ...... E	
	14 ...... Mimic	21 ...... A	
	15 I	22 ...... D	
	16 ...... W	23 ...... A	
	17 I	24 ...... B	
	18 ...... Method	25 ...... A	
	19 ...... S	26 ...... D	
	20 ...... R	27 C	
	21 ...... Mimic	28 ...... B	
	22 ...... S	29 ...... B	
	23 ...... S	30 C	
	24 ...... W	31 ...... B	
	25 ...... Mimic	32 C	
	26 ...... W	33 ...... E	
	27 ...... E	34 ...... B	
	28 I	35 C	
	29 ...... S	36 ...... A	
	30 ...... E	37 C	
		38 ...... A	
		39 C	
		40 ...... D	
		41 C	
		42 ...... A	
		43 ...... A	
		44 C	
		45 ...... D	

THE MBA TOUR
Your future begins here

The MBA Tour offers Quality Interaction With Top Business Schools

MEET with school representatives at our OPEN FAIR

LISTEN to top school experts discuss valuable MBA admission topics at our PANEL PRESENTATIONS

DISCUSS individual school qualities with representatives at our ROUNDTABLE EVENTS

ASIA
TOKYO

SEOUL

TAIPEI

BEIJING

SHANGHAI

BANGKOK

SINGAPORE

INDIA
BANGALORE

NEW DELHI

MUMBAI

UNITED STATES
HOUSTON

CHICAGO

ATLANTA

NEW YORK

BOSTON

WASHINGTON DC

LOS ANGELES

SAN FRANCISCO

SOUTH AMERICA
BUENOS AIRES

SANTIAGO

SAO PAULO

LIMA

BOGOTA

MEXICO CITY

EUROPE
MUNICH

LONDON

PARIS

CANADA
CALGARY

VANCOUVER

TORONTO

MONTREAL

Register at www.thembatour.com

THE MBA TOUR
Your future begins here